Table of Contents

Chapter 1 About REST

We can define Representational State Transfer (REST) as an architectural style that sits on top of a series of principles. The rise of REST in the last few years is tied to the API design that most web applications offer to extend their functionalities. Even if it is not tied to HTTP, REST is generally associated with web applications. HTTP happens to fit well with the REST principles.

The principles of REST are Uniform Interface, Stateless, Cacheable, Client-Server, Layered System, and Code on Demand.

This is a short introduction to REST architecture. What we need to understand is the basic principle and a general picture of a REST application. The idea of REST over HTTP is to use the protocol's functionality as much as possible so that we don't have to reinvent the wheel.

In the next chapters we will see how ASP.NET Web API helps in building web applications that match the REST constraints.

Uniform Interface

At the center of REST are the resources, the "things" that we want to manage using the API. A resource could be a blog post, a customer, a document, and in general, anything that we want to expose. A resource has an identifier, like a record in a database has a primary key. In the same way, a resource has a URI that identifies the resource itself. The URI is not a representation of the resource that can assume different formats. It is just an identifier that we can use to access the resource.

We can request the resource with the URI, and what we obtain is a representation of that requested resource in a particular format. The format is negotiated between the client and the server and could be anything from the most used XML and JSON, to HTML, PNG, CSV, or other binary formats. With the representation of the resource, the client can manipulate the state and operate with the resource using the server if it has the rights to do so.

Stateless

Statelessness is a fundamental principle for a REST application; the server should never store information about the clients. This means that when a request comes to the server, the server loads the resource from storage (typically a database) and sends back the representation to the client. That is the state of the resource. If a second later the state on the storage changes because of a new request that arrives, the client is not meant to know.

Stateless also means that the server should never use sessions or other mechanisms to store client information, and every request is not correlated with past or future requests.

Cacheable

The client can cache the resource, and the server should provide information about the cacheability of the resource itself. If we manage the cache correctly, we can save several trips to the server.

Client-Server

What the client sees is the URI and the representation of the resource—that's all. The client can't see (and surely isn't interested in seeing) where the resource is stored. On the other hand, the server should not know if the client has a particular resource, and if the interface doesn't change, internals of the server and client could change without breaking anything.

Layered System

The client knows very little about the server; it doesn't know, for example, if it is directly connected to the server or if it arrived at the server by passing through a proxy or other intermediary server (balancer, etc.).

Code on Demand

The server can extend the functionality of the client by passing executable code. For example, a server can send JavaScript to the client so that it can do some type of operation on the data.

If we read these principles carefully, we note that their primary focus is scalability. The fact that the server should not store client information permits it to save memory. The layered system permits us to use cache servers as a load balancer to obtain scalability. Adding new servers while adhering to the client-server principles allows us to change the implementation (for example, going from a SQL database to NoSQL storage) without the client's knowledge.

But how do we obtain this and how does it work? In the original paper outlining REST, Roy Fielding doesn't tie the REST architecture to HTTP, but as stated previously, HTTP seems perfect to build a REST API since most of the things that REST states are already built in the protocol itself (cacheability, for example).

The web itself is REST: we have the URL that is the identifier of the page that we need, we type the URL in the browser to obtain a representation in HTML format, and we use a link to transfer the state to another page.

An aspect of REST that contrasts with SOAP (RPC) is that the operation on the resource is based on the HTTP verb used in combination with the URI.

HTTP has the notion of verbs. We are used to GET and POST since the browser manages these two verbs, but others are specified in the HTTP specification (RFC 2616) that can be used for other operations.

The complete list of verbs is: OPTIONS, GET, HEAD, POST, PUT, PATCH, DELETE, TRACE, and CONNECT.

These can be used with their semantic meaning, so when we need to read a resource, we can use the GET method, and when we need to delete a resource, we can use a DELETE, and so on.

Table 1: HTTP verbs and meanings

Verb	URI	Description
GET	/posts	Get the post list.
GET	/posts/42	Get a single post (the one with id 42).
DELETE	/posts/42	Delete the post 42.
POST	/posts	Create a post.
PUT	/posts/42	Update the post.
PATCH	/post/42	Partial update.

OPTIONS	/post/42	Retrieve the available operation on the resource.
HEAD	/post/42	Return only the HTTP header.

As shown in the previous table, by using the right URI and the correct verb, we have the CRUD (Create, Read, Update, Delete) operations ready to be used.

After a request is issued to the server, the server parses it and builds the response to return the data or result to the client. Every response is represented with a state, and an HTTP status should be semantically used to inform the client of the result.

There are five types of HTTP status codes:

- Informational (1xx)
- Success (2xx)
- Redirection (3xx)
- Client errors (4xx)
- Server errors (5xx)

Every group has its own details. For example, if the request goes well, the status code of the response is 200 OK after a GET request, but is 201 CREATED after a POST request.

In the case of a client not authorized to issue a request, 403 Forbidden should be used; if a resource could not be found, a 404 Not found is used.

So, the general case is to find the HTTP status that best represents the current situation. The complete list of status codes can be found in Appendix A at the end of the book.

GET

The GET operation is used to read a resource. The URI specifies the resource that we are reading, and we can use the Accept header to ask for a specific format. For example, consider this HTTP request:

```
GET /posts HTTP/1.1

Accept: application/json
```

The GET request is instructing the server to return the content of the "posts" resource in JSON format.

```
GET /posts/42 HTTP/1.1

Accept: text/xml
```

This GET request asks the server to return a Post resource with an identifier of 42 in the XML format.

The GET operation is considered a safe one, so it should never modify the state of the resource.

The server generally responds to a GET request with the HTTP status 200 OK if everything goes well, 404 Not found if the URI points to a non-existent resource, or 400 Bad request if the request is not well formed.

POST

When POST is used to create a resource, the resource data is sent to the server as part of the request's body. The server responds with a status 201 CREATED if everything goes well. When a new resource is created, it's a best practice to use the Location header in the response to specify the URI of the newly created resource. This adheres to the HATEOAS principle.

HATEOAS (Hypermedia as the Engine of Application State)

In a REST application, the client needs to know as little information as possible to use the application. Ideally, the only thing the client needs to know is the URI of the entry point. All other URIs should be provided by the server using location headers or other mechanisms (rel links, for example) to inform the client where the other resources are. This way the client and the server are not tied and the server could change the location of the resource without breaking the client. This is at the base of the well-designed REST API.

PUT

PUT is used to modify the resource. The URI specifies the resource that we want to modify and the body contains the new resource values. The response HTTP status code should be 200 OK or 204 No content if the response doesn't contain the modified resource. It is not necessary to return the URI of the resource itself in the Location header because the client already knows it. PUT has to be idempotent, which means that the result of a successful request is independent of the number of times it is executed. It has to be possible to place two equal calls to the server, and the server should not return errors; the second call simply redoes the update even if it does not change the resource.

DELETE

DELETE is used to delete the resource. The result could be a 200 OK or 204 NO CONTENT if the response does not contain a body. It could be 404 Not Found if the URI is not correct and the resource cannot be found.

Summary

This is just a short introduction to REST, just what we need to correctly use the ASP.NET Web API. REST is a vast topic and entire books have been written about it. We just examined some principles and how the HTTP verbs are used to work with resources.

Chapter 2 Hello Web API

Hello World

Let's start by creating our first Web API project to see how it looks and to see what's inside.

The Web API template is part of the ASP.NET MVC 4 project template by default in Visual Studio 2012. For older versions of Visual Studio, you have to install the templates by downloading them from the http://asp.net website.

So let's create a new ASP.NET MVC 4 web application and in the second step choose the Web API template. Once created, the Web API project is almost identical to a classic ASP.NET MVC project, and in fact it keeps a lot of concepts from that kind of project.

Here it is: the solution structure as it appears after creating the project.

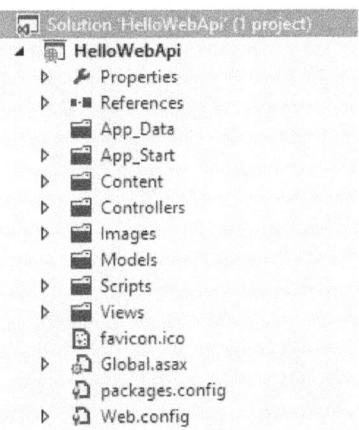

Figure 1: The Web API project structure

The most important things to note are:

- The Controllers, Models, and Views folders are taken from ASP.NET MVC. As we will see later, the Web API uses the same MVC pattern, so we will have controllers and models. There is a Views folder too, but it's not very useful in an API context, even if we could return a view to our caller.
- As well as the Views folder, there are Images, Scripts, and Content folders. These are not used often since an API is generally used to return data, not a user interface.
- The App_Start folder is used to configure the API. It contains various

configurators to set up the behavior of the API. This folder also contains some configuration for the ASP.NET MVC part.

As you can see with this project template, we could build ASP.NET MVC applications as well as Web API applications, since the two have a lot in common.

Let's go a little deeper by opening the **Controllers** folder and having a look at the `ValuesController` class:

```csharp
using System.Collections.Generic;
using System.Web.Http;


namespace HelloWebApi.Controllers
{
    public class ValuesController : ApiController
    {
        // GET api/values
        public IEnumerable<string> Get()
        {
            return new string[] { "value1", "value2" };
        }


        // GET api/values/5
        public string Get(int id)
        {
            return "value";
        }


        // POST api/values
        public void Post([FromBody]string value)
        {
        }


        // PUT api/values/5
        public void Put(int id, [FromBody]string value)
        {
        }
```

```
    // DELETE api/values/5

    public void Delete(int id)

    {

    }

    }

}
```

After the `using` and the `namespace`, we find a class declaration. The class `ValuesController` inherits from `ApiController`. This class is not relative to the controller base class used in ASP.NET MVC, even though it has a lot of similarities. It serves as a base class for all the resources that we decide to expose via the API.

Inside this class we find all the default verbs to manipulate the `value` resource: `GET`, `POST`, `PUT`, and `DELETE`. The name of the methods here matters, since the ASP.NET Web API runtime uses conventions to find the action to call against an HTTP request. So the two `Get(...)` methods are used to get a collection of values and to get a single value given its ID. The `Post(...)` and `Put(...)` are used to insert and modify the Value resource, while the `Delete(...)` method is used to delete a resource given the ID.

As you can see, the five methods are the actions that are called against a `GET`, `POST`, `PUT`, or `DELETE` HTTP request.

We will go further into conventions and other details about the previous code in the next chapters. For now we will focus on the overview of an ASP.NET Web API project.

Like an ASP.NET MVC web application, Web API projects use a routing system. The configuration of the routes is in a file called **WebApiConfig.cs** in the **App_Start** folder. Here is the content of that file:

```
using System.Web.Http;


namespace HelloWebApi

{

    public static class WebApiConfig

    {

        public static void Register(HttpConfiguration config)

        {

            config.Routes.MapHttpRoute(

                name: "DefaultApi",

                routeTemplate: "api/{controller}/{id}",

                defaults: new { id = RouteParameter.Optional }
```

```
        );

    }

  }

}
```

This class has one method that is invoked from the `WebApiApplication` class in the `global.asax`. This method registers the routes needed by the application. By default, the `ValuesController` defined before responds to the URI `/api/values`, as we can see in the previous code. Note that these routes, even though very similar to the ASP.NET MVC routes, are a completely different stack. In this case, the route type is `IHttpRoute` and the implementation is contained in the `system.web.Http` assembly, so it's completely new and is not tied to `system.Web`.

Even if they are different, they are implemented almost in the same way: each route has a name and a template that is tokenized to match the input patterns.

So until now, we have seen the `values` controller that has the duty to manage the `values` resource and a simple routing system to route the request to the matching controller. Let's run the Web API application to see how it works.

Once executed, it opens a local web server to a specific port. We can use a tool like Postman, which is a Chrome extension that works like an HTTP client.

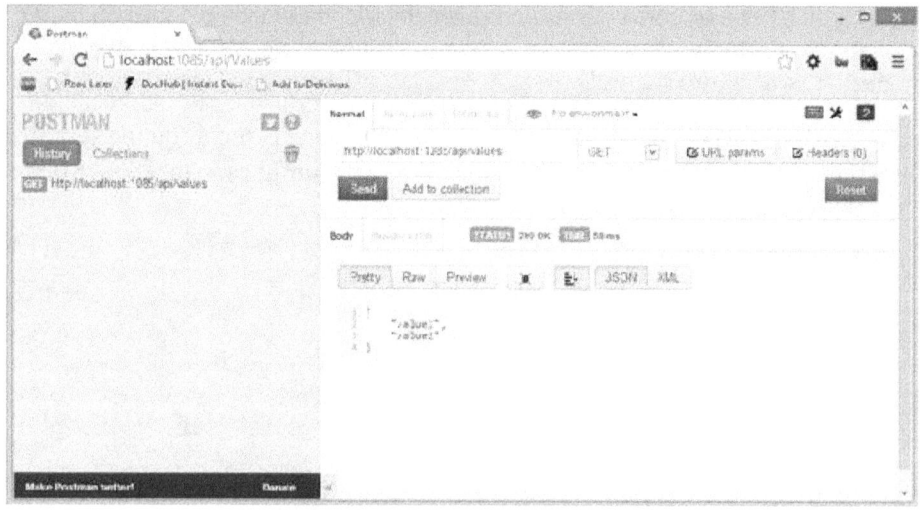

Figure 2: Executing a GET request

When we place a call to http://localhost:1085/api/values, the application responds with a `JSON` array that contains the two values defined in the controller.

The last thing that we could try is to change the `Accept` header to see what happens. In Postman, add a header to ask the server to give us `text/xml`:

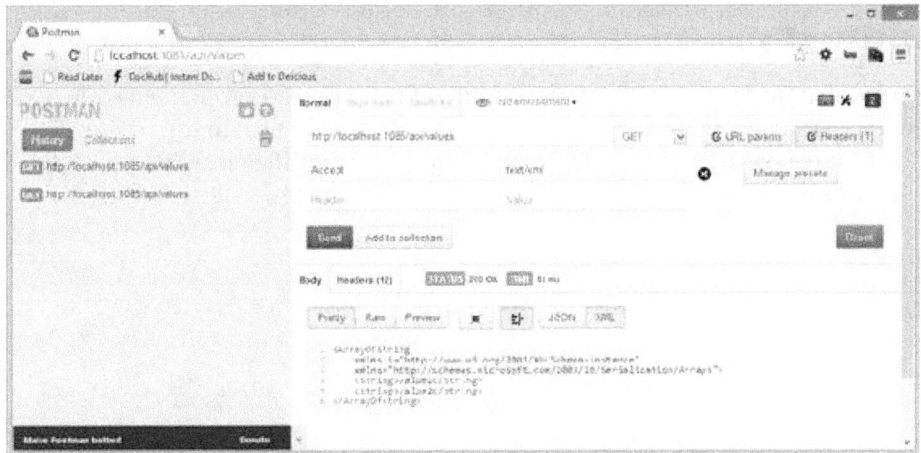

Figure 3: Executing a GET request specifying the accept header

What we obtain is an xmL response that contains the same two values. We don't need to change our code for these two types of responses since they are native in ASP.NET Web API.

Summary

We just had a quick look at the various parts of the Web API project template, and tried to run it to see what happens on the client. Now it is time to dig inside to understand the process model, the routes, and all the facilities that this ASP.NET Web API gives us.

Chapter 3 The Life of a Request

Processing a request

When a client sends a request to an ASP.NET Web API application, there are three layers that process the request. The main components that play an active role in this route are shown in the following figure:

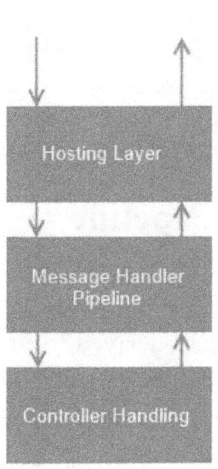

Figure 4: Steps in Request Processing

Let's see what happens at each stage.

Down the rabbit hole

Consider a request that is issued from a client and reaches the first layer.

The Hosting Layer

The first layer is the hosting layer, which receives the HTTP request directly from the client. The hosting layer could be a classic Internet Information Server that uses the ASP.NET pipeline, or a self-hosted application (we will talk more about self-hosting in Chapter 11).

The role of the hosting layer is to receive the requests and convert them into instances of `HttpRequestMessage`, a class that represents the request. This request message is passed down to the Message Handler Pipeline. How this request is built depends on the hosting type, but for now we won't go any further.

The Message Handler Pipeline

The message handler pipeline represents the middleware of our architecture. It consists of a chain of handlers that are pluggable to meet the needs of the application. Each handler is an instance of a class derived from `HttpMessageHandler` that has one method, `SendAsync`, which receives an instance of `HttpRequestMessage` and returns an `HttpResponseMessage`.

Each of these handlers has a reference to an `InnerHandler`, the next handler in the chain that will be called in sequence.

With this architecture, each request can be pre-processed or post-processed by multiple handlers doing different things.

Examples of message handlers are the `HttpRoutingDispatcher` that dispatches the request based on the route and the `HttpControllerDispatcher` that sends the request to the controller.

These handlers are already on the chain, as they are in the collection `HttpConfiguration.MessageHandlers`. Others can be added to the collection during the configuration of the Web API application.

The two handlers that we previously mentioned are the two special handlers at the end of the chain.

Controller Handling

We are now at the bottom of the route. The controller handling layer receives the request message from the layer above it and calls the action on the controller passing the required parameters. The task is accomplished by the `HttpControllerDispatcher`, the last handler in the chain. This, with the help of `HttpControllerDescriptor`, obtains an instance of a class that implements the `IHttpInterface` and calls the method `ExecuteAsync` on this instance. Selecting the correct action to execute is the job of the `ApiController.ExecuteAsync` method, which binds the parameters, executes the action filters (if they are present), and executes the action itself.

An `IActionResultConverter` converts the result of the action to an instance of `HttpResponseMessage`. The response message goes up to the client following the same path as the request.

Summary

In this chapter we took a quick look at the main components that compose the ASP.NET Web API and the role of these components. In the next chapters we will go inside each of these modules to understand how they are implemented and how we can use them to build our applications.

Chapter 4 The Routing System

Basic routing

All HTTP requests pass through the routing system, which decides what will manage the request. The main task of the routing system is to decide which action of which controller should be called to manage the actual request. To make this decision, the routing system parses the HTTP request (in particular, the verb and the URI), and obtains a series of tokens that are matched to a route table containing all the possible routes.

As we saw in Chapter 2, when we create a new Web API application, the template generates one default route for us:

```
using System.Web.Http;


namespace HelloWebApi
{

    public static class WebApiConfig
    {

        public static void Register(HttpConfiguration config)
        {

            config.Routes.MapHttpRoute(

                name: "DefaultApi",

                routeTemplate: "api/{controller}/{id}",

                defaults: new { id = RouteParameter.Optional }

            );

        }

    }

}
```

The method `MapHttpRoute` in this case takes three parameters:

- A route name (`DefaultApi`).
- A route template: A template with a literal (`api`) and two placeholders (`controller` and `id`) that will be replaced with the current request segments.
- Default values: In this case, we are saying that the `id` is not mandatory in the request.

If you have used ASP.NET MVC, you will find several similarities. In MVC, however, you should have the action, and here the action is not present. This is the main difference between the two routing systems. In Web API, the action is determined by the HTTP method, as we will see later.

The MapHttpRoute method simply adds a new entry in a dictionary that stores all the routes. The route that we have just defined, given that we have defined a PostsController, will respond to these requests:

- /api/Posts
- /api/Posts/42
- /api/Posts/Syncfusion

If the routing system does not find a correct match, it will return HTTP status 404 Not Found to the caller.

To decide which action should be called, the routing system must analyze the HTTP method. If we place a GET request to the server, the action should be something like GetSomeResource(...). If we place a POST, the action should be something like PostSomeOtherResource(...). The general rule for the default methods is that the action must start with the action name, so if we consider a GET HTTP request then Get(...), GetPosts(...), and GetSomething(...) are all valid actions.

The complete route table for the previous route follows:

Table 2: A route table

HTTP method	URI	Controller	Action	Parameter
GET	/api/Posts	PostsController	Get()	N/A
GET	/api/Posts/42	PostsController	Get(int id)	42
POST	/api/Posts	PostsController	Post(Post c)	From the body
DELETE	/api/Posts/42	PostsController	Delete(int id)	42

The route that Visual Studio defines for us can be changed and we are not forced to use it, even if it is a general best practice for every REST service.

When modifying or adding new routes, consider that the route table is evaluated in the order that the routes are added. So the first match will be used.

Consider this example:

```
using System.Web.Http;


namespace HelloWebApi

{
```

```
public static class WebApiConfig
{
    public static void Register(HttpConfiguration config)
    {
        config.Routes.MapHttpRoute(
            name: "PostByDate",
            routeTemplate: "api/{controller}/{year}/{month}/{day}",
            defaults: new { month = RouteParameter.Optional, day = RouteParameter.Optional }
        );

        config.Routes.MapHttpRoute(
            name: "DefaultApi",
            routeTemplate: "api/{controller}/{id}",
            defaults: new { id = RouteParameter.Optional }
        );
    }
}
```

Here we have a new route defined before the default one; this means that the route named PostByDate is evaluated before the other. This new route has four placeholders: one for the controller name, and three to define a date (year, month, and day). In the defaults value parameter, we specify that month and day are optional but year remains mandatory.

To see the example working, we define a new PostsController like this:

```
using System.Web.Http;

namespace HelloWebApi
{
    public class PostsController : ApiController
    {
        public IQueryable<Post> Get(int year, int month = 0, int day = 0)
        {
            // Do something to load the posts that match the date.
        }
    }
}
```

}

The Get method takes three parameters: a year (mandatory), and a month and a day that are optional (if not given, they will contain the default value of the given type, which in our case is zero).

The request will be parsed and decomposed to be able to call the Get action with its parameters:

Table 3: Request URI and parameters value

URI	Year	Month	Day
GET /api/Posts/2010/04/11	2010	4	11
GET /api/Posts/1977/11	1977	11	0
Get /api/Posts/1973	1973	0	0

As you can see, with this simple route we have defined a REST interface to query posts based on the date, which can be a precise day, a particular month, or a full year.

We have to define two more things to be sure that everything is correct.

First, a route like this is generally used with a single controller. It's quite strange that every resource could be queried with a date, so it would be better to create a tight link between the route and the controller. This can be done in this way:

```
// ...

config.Routes.MapHttpRoute(

    name: "PostByDate",

    routeTemplate: "api/Posts/{year}/{month}/{day}",

    defaults: new

        {

            controller = "Posts",

            month = RouteParameter.Optional,

            day = RouteParameter.Optional

        }

    );
// ...
```

We could simply remove the controller placeholder and use the literal "Posts" so the route will match only if the request contains the posts string (it's case insensitive).

The other problem is that this route does not impose any constraints on the parameters, so this URI:

```
/api/Posts/2013/May
```

is being caught even if it breaks the action, since the month is a string and nothing manages the conversion.

To be sure that the parameters are numbers, we could use a route constraint as in the following code:

```
// ...

config.Routes.MapHttpRoute(

    name: "PostByDate",

    routeTemplate: "api/Posts/{year}/{month}/{day}",

    defaults: new

        {

            controller = "Posts",

            month = RouteParameter.Optional,

            day = RouteParameter.Optional

        },

    constraints: new

        {

            month = @"\d{0,2}", day = @"\d{0,2}"

        }

    );

// ...
```

The constraints parameter uses a regular expression to be sure that month and day are two numbers (composed of zero, one, or two digits).

As specified previously, the controller's action that has to be executed is selected by the HTTP method, so we have only seven actions available. What happens if I want more actions or a custom action name that does not start with Get, Post, and so on?

One way to achieve this behavior is to use the placeholder `action` in the route definition:

```
// ...

config.Routes.MapHttpRoute(

    name: "PostsCustomAction",

    routeTemplate: "api/{controller}/{action}/{id}",

    defaults: new { id = RouteParameter.Optional }

    );

// ...
```

Given this route definition, the action will be explicitly written in the URL, so we are not forced to use the seven default actions. But we can use a URL like:

`/api/Posts/Category/10`

that will be managed by the action `Category` in the `Posts` controller, but this member must have an attribute that specifies the method that it supports:

```
public class PostsController : ApiController
{

    [HttpGet]

    public string Category(int id)

    {

        // ...

    }

}
```

The `HttpGet` attribute is there to tell the runtime that the action `Category` should be called only against an HTTP `GET` method.

If we try to `POST` to this URL we obtain the following error:

The requested resource does not support http method 'POST'

The possible attributes that match all the HTTP methods are:

- HttpGet
- HttpPost
- HttpPut
- HttpOptions
- HttpPatch
- HttpDelete
- HttpHead

Summary

With all these options, we have all that is needed to define a complete route table that satisfies all our requests. When designing a route table, always keep in mind the readability of the URLs that represent an important part of our user interface.

Chapter 5 The Controller

Controller basics

The Controller is the main element in the resource management since it represents the operations on the resource exposed to the client. All the Web API controllers must implement the IHttpController interface, and in general they inherit from ApiController. ApiController is an abstract class that exposes some basic functionality to all the controllers, and implements IHttpController.

The ApiController interface is reported here:

```
public class ApiController
{

    HttpRequestMessage Request { /* */ }

    HttpConfiguration Configuration { /* */ }

    HttpControllerContext ControllerContext { /* */}

    ModelStateDictionary ModelState { /* */}

    UrlHelper Url { /* */}

    IPrincipal User { /* */ }

    Task<HttpResponseMessage> ExecuteAsync(HttpControllerContext controllerContext, CancellationToken cancellationToken){ /* */ }

    void Dispose() {/* */ }

}
```

As mentioned previously, the entry point for the controller is the ExecuteAsync method that is in charge of selecting the action and executing it. The action selection is based on the HTTP method, so if there is a GET request, the controller will search for a public instance method that starts with Get, or for those with the HttpGet attribute.

When executing the selected action, the controller executes the filters pipeline; if there is any filter it will be executed before the action itself.

Considering a blog post resource, the controller that will manage it will be something like this:

```
public class PostsController : ApiController
{

    private readonly IPostRepository _repository;


    public PostsController(IPostRepository repository)
```

```csharp
{
    _repository = repository;
}

public IQueryable<Post> Get()
{
    return _repository.GetAll();
}

public Post Get(int id)
{
    return _repository.Get(id);
}

public HttpResponseMessage Post(Post post)
{
    _repository.Create(post);
    var response = Request.CreateResponse(HttpStatusCode.Created);
    response.StatusCode = HttpStatusCode.Created;
    string uri = Url.Link("DefaultApi", new { id = post.Id });
    response.Headers.Location = new Uri(uri);

    return response;
}

public HttpResponseMessage Put(int id, Post post)
{
    post.Id = id;
    _repository.Update(post);
    var response = Request.CreateResponse(HttpStatusCode.NoContent);
    string uri = Url.Link("DefaultApi", new { id = post.Id });
    response.Headers.Location = new Uri(uri);
    return response;
}
```

```
public HttpResponseMessage Delete(int id)
{
    _repository.Delete(id);

    var response = Request.CreateResponse(HttpStatusCode.NoContent);

    return response;
}
}
```

It exposes the five typical methods used to do the CRUD operations. Each method has its own signature, and other than reading and persisting data using the repository, it enriches the response with headers and other things where necessary.

In the previous example, we omitted the error-checking to keep the code focused on the REST API. We will see how to manage the errors later in this chapter.

Let's go deeper in every method to understand what happens.

Actions

Get()

Actually, there are two overloads of Get: one that returns the entire collection of posts, and one that returns a single post. The first one will simply build an IQueryable collection of posts (we will return to the meaning of IQueryable later).

```
public IQueryable<Post> Get()
{

    return _repository.GetAll();

}
```

This method is quite easy; it simply asks the repository to return a collection of available Posts without filters or other selection clauses, and then returns the collection (IQueryable<Post>) to the caller.

As we said before, the result of the controller should be an HttpResponseMessage. What happens when the action returns a model object like Post?

The method in the base ApiController that calls the Get method wraps the result in an HttpResponseMessage, putting the Post object inside the content. So we have two ways of returning results to the client:

- Build the HttpResponseMessage directly.
- Return an object and let the ASP.NET Web API create the HttpResponseMessage response for us.

Typically, if there is no need to manipulate the response (headers, statuses, etc.), the easiest way to return results is to return the objects directly, as we did in the previous code example.

To call this method, we have to issue a GET request to the URI /api/Posts without any other parameters.

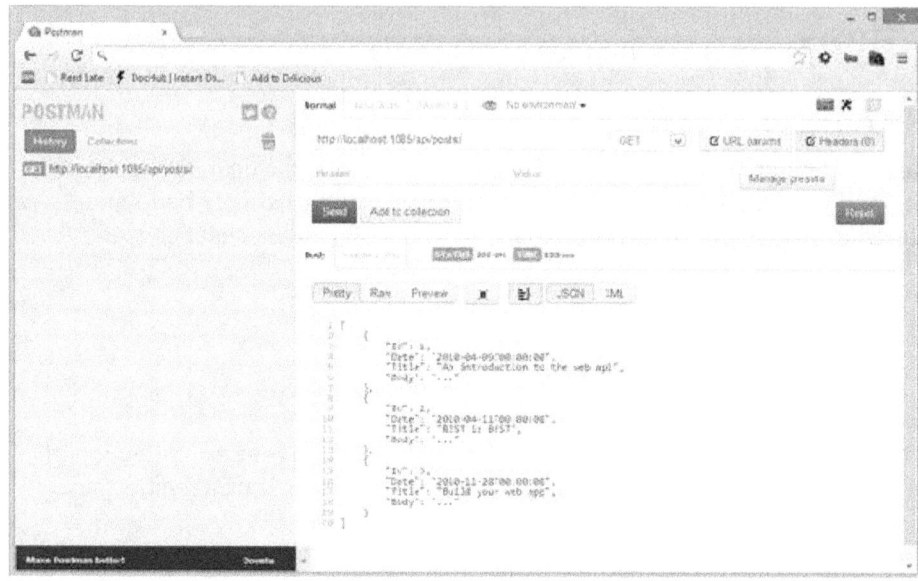

Figure 5: A simple get

With the help of Postman we can inspect the response. The status is 200 ok. If everything is okay, the ASP.NET Web API pipeline adds the HTTP status for us, and in this case 200 ok is what we expect. In the body we can see the list of the Post objects returned by the controller. As we can see, the format is json; this is the default format if no header is specified in the request.

Postman

Postman is a Chrome extension that helps you be more efficient while working with APIs. It helps you in building HTTP requests with parameters, headers, authentication, and so on. It sends the request and reads the response. It is an open source project. More info can be found on the official site: http://www.getpostman.com

---

Get(int id)

This is the second type of GET where we specify the Id of the resource that we want.

```
public Post Get(int id)
{
    return _repository.Get(id);
}
```

The code is quite similar to the previous case, and the only difference is that here the action returns a single Post rather than a collection. Here again is the ApiController that wraps the returned post into an HttpResponseMessage and sets the headers and status codes (in this case, 200 ok as in the previous case).

Post (Post post)

Here is where things get interesting. The `Post()` method has the aim to create a new `Post` in the storage and to return the correct status code to the caller.

```csharp
public HttpResponseMessage Post(Post post)
{
    _repository.Create(post);

    HttpResponseMessage response = Request.CreateResponse(HttpStatusCode.Created);

    response.StatusCode = HttpStatusCode.Created;

    string uri = Url.Link("DefaultApi", new { id = post.Id });

    response.Headers.Location = new URI(uri);


    return response;
}
```

To store the `Post`, we use the `Create()` method of the `PostRepository`, which will save the post to the defined storage. In this case, the response message has to be created manually in order to be able to set some attributes and to build the correct response from a REST point of view.

To create the response message we use the method `CreateResponse()`, passing the status code for this kind of request (`201 Created`).

Then we add the location header that will contain the URI of the newly created resource. To do this, we simply need to set the value of the `response.Headers.Location` attribute with the URI of the new `Post`. To build the URI, instead of writing it manually, we use the URL helper and we pass the route name (`DefaultApi`) and the `Post.Id` to the `Link` method. This method will return something like `/api/Posts/42`, where `42` is the `id` of the newly created `Post`.

With Postman, we create a new `HTTP POST` request specifying the information about the `Post` object in the request body.

The response body will be empty since we don't return any value, only the status (`201 Created`) and the new location of the object. The interesting part is the headers.

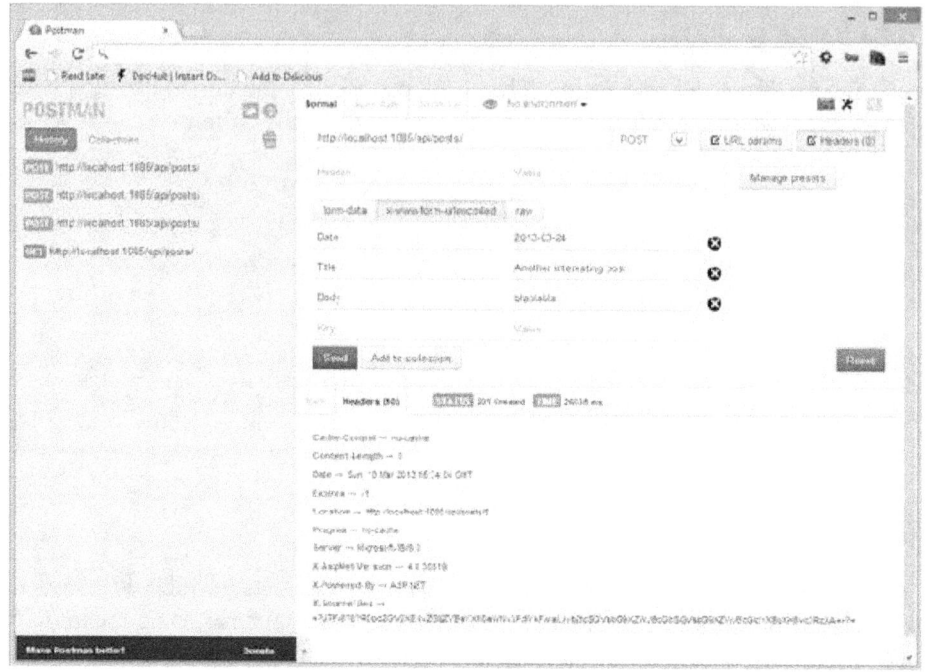

Figure 6: A POST

In Figure 6, we can see that the header location points to the newly created `Post` with an `id` equal to 5. By specifying the new location, the client application will be automatically informed about the location of the new object rather than guessing and manually constructing the URI; that is exactly what we need to build a real Hypermedia API.

If we want to see how the newly created `Post` looks, we just need to issue a `GET` request to the location URI `/api/posts/5`:

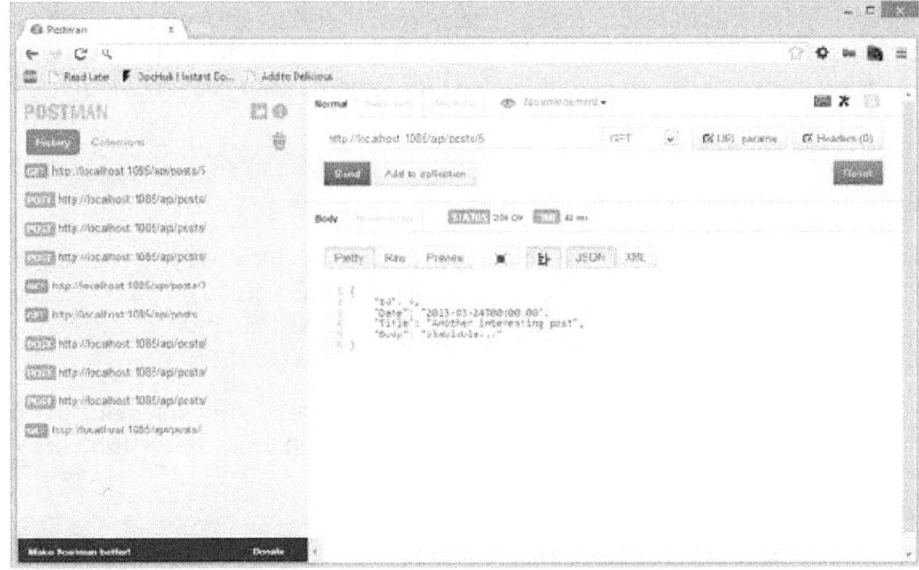

Figure 7: A GET request to the newly created resource

Put (int id, Post post)

The Put() action is used to change the resource. This method takes two parameters: one that comes from the URI (the id) and the second that is specified in the request body (the Post object itself). As the Put() method acts against a resource, we need to have the Id in the URI (as when we used the GET method /api/posts/5). The Id will represent the resource to be modified, and the request body will contain the new content of the Post to be stored.

```
public HttpResponseMessage Put(int id, Post post)
{
    post.Id = id;
    _repository.Update(post);
    var response = Request.CreateResponse(HttpStatusCode.OK, post);
    string uri = Url.Link("DefaultApi", new { id = post.Id });
    response.Headers.Location = new URI(uri);
    return response;
}
```

The implementation of the Put() method is similar to the Post() method. The difference is in the response status code: it is 200 OK, and the response contains the updated post (the call to CreateResponse takes the status and the content).

Putting the updated `Post` object inside the response is a matter of preference. Sometimes `PUT` has an empty body and contains only the location header to the updated resource. In this case, we decided to include the updated `Post` even if not strictly necessary.

To include the post inside the response we use an overload of the `CreateResponse()` method, passing the instance of a `Post` in addition to the status code.

When we try to call the resource with a `PUT`, by HTTP standards we need to pass the full content of a resource that needs to be modified. If we were to do partial updates the preferred way is to use either `PATCH` (more information about PATCH can be found at http://www.rfc-editor.org/rfc/rfc5789.txt) or `POST` verbs.

Therefore, if we pass in the body the new title, the response will contain the full post with the new title, and the location header we specified in the action will be in the headers.

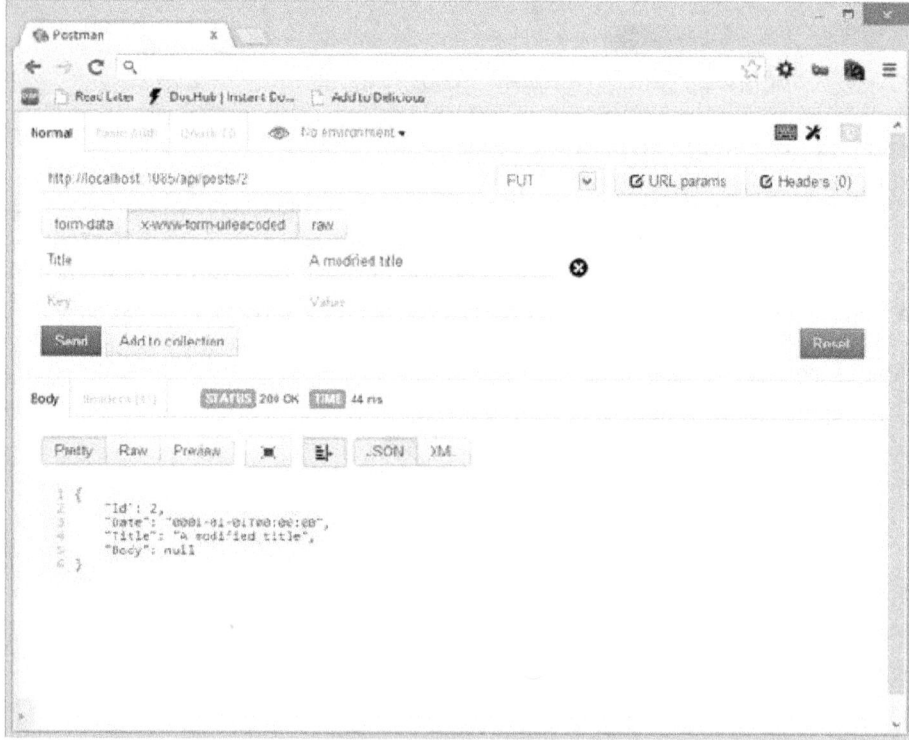

Figure 8: A PUT

Delete(int id)

The last action is the `DELETE` method.

```
public HttpResponseMessage Delete(int id)
{
    _repository.Delete(id);
    HttpResponseMessage response = Request.CreateResponse(HttpStatusCode.NoContent);
    return response;
}
```

We simply delete the given post using the repository and return an empty response to the client. No specific header has to be specified. We have used the 203 No Content HTTP status to specify that the response has no body.

Custom Actions

Until now we saw the classic five actions that perform the CRUD operations, and each method begins with the HTTP method name. What if we need other methods?

We can use the action attributes to specify the HTTP method that matches the request.

Consider the following example: We would like to add an action to view the posts using a date, and we'd like to have a group of URIs like these:

Table 4: URL and descriptions

/api/posts/archive/2010/04/11	Returns all the posts of 11 April 2010
/api/posts/archive/2010/04	Returns all the posts of April 2010
/api/posts/archive/2010	Returns all the posts of 2010

We first need to define a new route for the archive action:

```
config.Routes.MapHttpRoute(

    name: "Archive",

    routeTemplate: "api/posts/archive/{year}/{month}/{day}",

    defaults: new {

                controller = "Posts",

                month = RouteParameter.Optional,

                day = RouteParameter.Optional

            },

    constraints: new { month = @"\d{0,2}", day = @"\d{0,2}"}

);
```

This code defines a new route with three parameters: year, month, and day. It is assigned to the PostsController, and the month and day must be numbers.

With this route, we can define a new method in the PostsController class that responds to this route:

```
[HttpGet]

public IQueryable<Post> Archive(int year, int month = 0, int day = 0)

{

    return _repository.Search(year, month, year);

}
```

This action simply takes the three parameters and issues a query using the repository. Note that month and day have a default value since they are not mandatory in the request.

This action is decorated with the `HttpGetAttribute` that is needed to route the request since the method name does not start with `Get`.

 Note: Another solution would be to rename the method as GetArchive so that it matches the default convention.

Model Binding

In the previous example, we saw an action like this:

```
public HttpResponseMessage Post(Post post)
{
    /* ...some code here... */
}
```

How is the `Post` parameter built?

If we analyze the request, we will see something like this:

```
POST http://localhost:1085/api/posts HTTP/1.1

Host: localhost:1085

Connection: keep-alive

Content-Length: 51

Cache-Control: no-cache

User-Agent: Mozilla/5.0 (Windows NT 6.2; WOW64) AppleWebKit/537.22 (KHTML, like Geck
o) Chrome/25.0.1364.152 Safari/537.22

Content-Type: application/x-www-form-urlencoded

Accept: */*

Accept-Encoding: gzip,deflate,sdch

Accept-Language: en-US,en;q=0.8,it;q=0.6

Accept-Charset: ISO-8859-1,utf-8;q=0.7,*;q=0.3


Title=Hello+again&Date=2013-04-20&Body=hi+everybody!
```

We could see at the end of the post request the collection of values (the body of the request):

```
Title=Hello+again&Date=2013-04-20&Body=hi+everybody!
```

A parameter's so-called *model binder* converts this body to a `Post` object. The task of a model binder is to parse the request and extract from it the values that the action needs. By default, there are two model binders that operate in different ways: `ModelBinderParameterBinding` and `FormatterParameterBinding`.

These classes inherit from the abstract class `HttpParameterBinding` and implement their behavior in the method `ExecuteBindingAsync`. The `ModelBinderParameterBinding` is the preferred method since it extracts the values from the URI (route parameters or query string), while `FormatterParameterBinding` uses a `MediaTypeFormatter` (more on this in the next chapter) to parse the body and build complex objects.

Inside the class ModelBinderParameterBinding are the ValueProviders. These objects aggregate values from various elements of the incoming request (Header, QueryString, Body, and so on). The ModelBinder uses these ValueProviders to build the model.

To better understand how all this works, let us look at an example. Suppose that we need to extract an action parameter from a header. To do this, we need to implement an IValueProvider:

```
public class HeaderValueProvider : IValueProvider
{
    public HttpRequestHeaders Headers { get; set; }

    public HeaderValueProvider(HttpRequestHeaders headers)
    {
        Headers = headers;
    }


    public bool ContainsPrefix(string prefix)
    {
        return Headers.Any(s => s.Key.StartsWith(prefix));
    }


    public ValueProviderResult GetValue(string key)
    {
        KeyValuePair<string, IEnumerable<string>> header = Headers.FirstOrDefault(s => s.Key.Sta
rtsWith(key));

        string headerValue = string.Join(",", header.Value);

        return new ValueProviderResult(headerValue, headerValue, CultureInfo.InvariantCulture);
    }
}
```

This class has two methods worth mentioning. The ContainsPrefix method is called to verify that the header contains the information that we need, where the prefix string is usually the name of the action parameter. The GetValue method is called to extract the information from the header and to return it in a form of ValueProviderResult.

To link this provider to our action, we need to use an attribute:

```
public HttpResponseMessage Post([ValueProvider(typeof(HeaderValueFactory))] String username)
{
```

```
//...
}
```

Since the `ValueProviderAttribute` needs a `ValueProviderFactory`, our last task is to implement a factory that builds our `HeaderValueProvider`:

```
public class HeaderValueFactory : ValueProviderFactory
{
    public override IValueProvider GetValueProvider(HttpActionContext actionContext)
    {
        return new HeaderValueProvider(actionContext.Request.Headers);
    }
}
```

This completes the necessary classes to build a binder that extracts the value from the header. As we can see it is not so easy and it requires a lot of tasks; fortunately, the default binders are usually smart enough in de-serializing the request and creating the correct parameters for your actions.

Remember that by default for the primitive types and `DateTime`, `TimeSpan`, `Guid`, `Decimal`, and `string`, the ASP.NET Web API uses model binding and extracts the values from the URI. If we need to, we can override the default behavior using the attribute `FromBody` to specify that the value came from the body:

```
public HttpResponseMessage Post([FromBody] String username)
```

In other particular cases, we can use the `ModelBinder` attribute to specify that we need a specific implementation of `ModelBinder`:

```
public HttpResponseMessage Post([ModelBinder(typeof(UserModelBinder))] User username)
```

With the `ModelBinder` attribute, we can specify the implementation of `IModelBinder` that builds the `User` parameter:

```
public interface IModelBinder
{
    object BindModel(ControllerContext cc, ModelBindingContext mbc);
}
```

It's the method `BindModel` that builds the instance of `User` that will be passed to the `Post` action.

Let us see the different ways in which the parameters are bound to our actions. By default, ASP.NET Web API tries to get simple values from the query string or the route parameters. So, for example, if the request URL is something like this:

```
/?tag=web&date=20130409
```

Both `tag` and `date` are taken from the URI so there is no need to specify custom binders or attributes.

If we force using the attribute to a parameter, the parameter is read from the body:

```
void Action([FromBody] string name);
```

Instead, if we do not specify other attributes and we have an action with one simple type and one complex type, the first is read from the URI while the complex type will be taken from the body:

```
void Action(int id, Post p)
```

`id` will be taken from the URI, and `Post` from the body, since it is a complex type.

If we have an action that takes two complex types, one must come from the body while the other must come from another source:

```
void Action([FromUri] Customer c1, Customer c2)
```

`c1` is from the URI and `c2` is from the body

In any case, we can define a custom model binder and use an attribute to specify that we want to use it:

```
void Action([ModelBinder(PostCustomBinder)] Post p)
```

The `PostCustomModelBinder` will be used to build a post instance.

Note: One important thing to remember is that the Web API reads the response body at most once, so only one parameter of an action can come from the request body. If you need to get multiple values from the request body, define a complex type. If your action needs multiple complex types, only one should come from the body.

This means that this action:

```
public HttpResponseMessage Post(Post post, User user)
```

will raise an `InvalidOperationException: Can't bind multiple parameters ('post' and 'user') to the request's content.`

To make sure that this action works, we need to use an attribute to specify that `Post` (or `User`) comes from URI:

```
public HttpResponseMessage Post(Post post, [FromUri]User user)
```

The `FromUri` attribute forces the parsing of the user from the URI instead of the body.

Summary

The controller is the heart of the ASP.NET Web API. It is where programmers spend most of their time, and it's where the cooperation between the input and the models and services takes place.

In this chapter, we saw what a controller is and what kind of operations it exposes, from default actions to custom actions. Then we saw how the model binders operate to transform the request data into action parameters.

Chapter 6 Model Validation

The attributes

As in ASP.NET, MVC models can be validated when they enter the Web API pipeline. To define the validation, our model must be decorated with attributes from the namespace `System.ComponenModel.DataAnnotations`. Considering our `Post` model, we can add validation specifying attributes like this:

```
public class Post
{
    public int Id { get; set; }

    public DateTime Date { get; set; }

    [Required]
    public string Title { get; set; }

    [Required]
    public string Body { get; set; }
}
```

In this example, we added the attribute `Required` to `Title` and `Body` to specify that a `Post` must always have a `Title` and a `Body`.

ModelState

These attributes affect the `ModelState` property of the `Controller` class.

```
public HttpResponseMessage Post(Post post)
{

    if (ModelState.IsValid)
    {

        // ...normal execution...

    }

    else
    {

        return new HttpResponseMessage(HttpStatusCode.BadRequest);

    }

}
```

The `ModelState` object is a `Dictionary` that contains a list of errors that can be used to check the model if contains errors.

With the `Post` model decorated as before, if we issue a post that breaks the required attributes, the `ModelState` will contain the list of errors and the property `IsValid` is set to `false`.

For example, if we post a `Post` without the body attribute, the `ModelState` will be something like this:

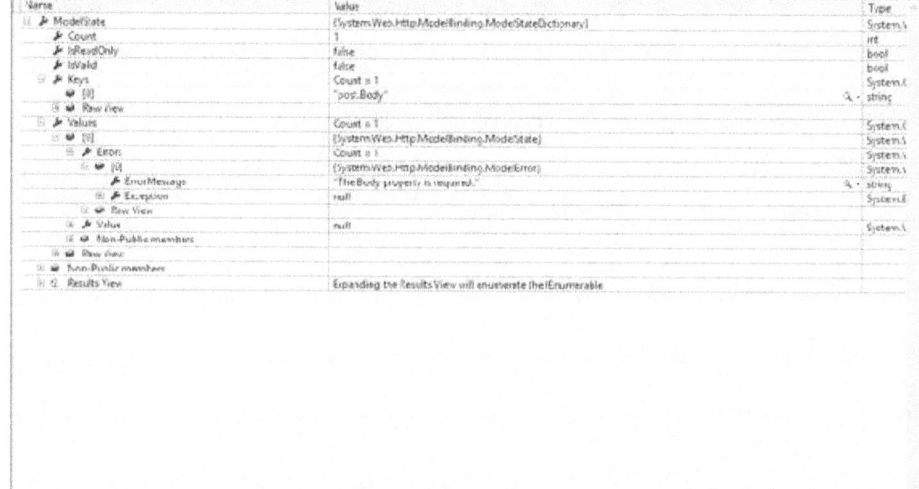

Figure 9: The ModelState is invalid

It contains the list of Keys and Values that do not pass the validation. The errors are a list of ModelErrors that contains the error messages and other information. We can use the error messages to build a response so that the client will know which attributes do not match the validation. In the case of a validation error, we should return an HTTP Status 400 Bad request.

The following table shows the actual built-in attributes:

Table 5: Current built-in validation attributes

Attribute	Description
CompareAttribute	Provides an attribute that compares two properties.
CustomValidationAttribute	Specifies a custom validation method that is used to validate a property or class instance.
DataTypeAttribute	Specifies the name of an additional type to associate with a data field.
MaxLengthAttribute	Specifies the maximum length of array or string data allowed in a property.
MinLengthAttribute	Specifies the minimum length of array or string data allowed in a property.
RangeAttribute	Specifies the numeric range constraints for the value of a data field.
RegularExpressionAttribute	Specifies that a data field value in ASP.NET Dynamic Data must match the specified regular expression.
RequiredAttribute	Specifies that a data field value is required.
StringLengthAttribute	Specifies the minimum and maximum length of characters that are allowed in a data field.

This is the basic list of validators that inherit from ValidationAttribute. With the advent of .NET Framework 4.0, others were added as DataValidator, a subclass of ValidationAttribute that is used to derive a sort of type validator. These are listed in the following table:

Table 6: DataType attributes

Attribute	Description
CreditCardAttribute	Specifies that a data field value is a credit card number.

EmailAddressAttribute	Validates an email address.
EnumDataTypeAttribute	Enables a .NET Framework enumeration to be mapped to a data column.
FileExtensionsAttribute	Validates file name extensions.
PhoneAttribute	Specifies that a data field value is a well-formed phone number using a regular expression for phone numbers.
UrlAttribute	Provides URL validation.

The attributes can be customized and personalized by deriving from the existing ones, or we can build new attributes that contain strong logic to validate the data. The base class from which we must derive is `ValidationAttribute`.

Summary

In this chapter, we saw how to use the validation mechanism to validate our models without modifying the existing code. This is just another tool to keep in our library.

Chapter 7 Content Negotiation

Formatting a resource

As we already know from Chapter 1, the client can ask for the resource in a specific format using the `Accept` header. With this, the server will try to serve the request to match the specific format and if the format is not supported, it returns a `406 Not Acceptable`.

The Web API uses a content negotiation mechanism to support this functionality. We saw in the previous chapter that all the responses are served as `JSON`, but we can ask for `XML` format too.

Consider the `Post` example and build a request like this:

Figure 10: A GET that specifies the accept type

We simply add the `Accept` header and set it to `text/xml`. This means that the client asks for the `Post` with an `Id` equal to `1` in `XML` format. In fact, the server responds with an `XML` response with elements that match the attributes of the `Post` object.

This works because the ASP.NET Web API has the `XmlFormatter` included in the list of available formatters.

Formatters are objects that inherit from `MediaTypeFormatter`, an abstract class with the following interface:

```
public abstract class MediaTypeFormatter
{
    Collection<MediaTypeHeaderValue> SupportedMediaTypes { get; }

    Collection<Encoding> SupportedEncodings { get; }

    Collection<MediaTypeMapping> MediaTypeMappings { get; }

    IRequiredMemberSelector RequiredMemberSelector { get; set; }

    Task<object> ReadFromStreamAsync(Type type, Stream readStream, HttpContent content, IFormatterLogger formatterLogger);

    Task WriteToStreamAsync(Type type, object value, Stream writeStream, HttpContent content, TransportContext transportContext);

    Encoding SelectCharacterEncoding(HttpContentHeaders contentHeaders);

    void SetDefaultContentHeaders(Type type, HttpContentHeaders headers, MediaTypeHeaderValue mediaType);

    MediaTypeFormatter GetPerRequestFormatterInstance(Type type, HttpRequestMessage request, MediaTypeHeaderValue mediaType);

    bool CanReadType(Type type);

    bool CanWriteType(Type type);
}
```

At first look, we could see that a formatter can read and write data. This makes sense because a formatter can parse the request in a specific format to build the parameters for the actions, and on the other side can convert the result of an action to another specific format.

Given that the most important members are:

- **SupportedMediaType**: A collection of the types supported by this formatter. These correspond to the MIME types of the requests.
- **CanReadType**: A Boolean that is true if the formatter is able to read the type from the request.
- **CanWriteType**: A Boolean that is true if the formatter is able to write the type to the response.
- **ReadFromStreamAsync**: This is the method that will be called to read from the input stream. It should return the instance of the resource.
- **WriteToStreamAsync**: This is the method that will be called to write the resource to the output stream.

In the ASP.NET Web API, there are already four media type formatters out-of-the-box:

- **JsonMediaTypeFormatter**: Format the requested resource in JSON format (this is the default formatter).

- `XmlMediaTypeFormatter`: Format the requested resource in xml format.
- `FormUrlEncodedMediaTypeFormatter`: This is used to manage the application/x-www-form-urlencoded requests.
- `JQueryMvcFormUrlEncodedFormatter`: Derives from the `FormURLEncodedMediaTypeFormatter` and adds support for the JQuerySchema.

If we want, we can add our own formatters to match the API specification.

Let's look at an example to see what we can do with a media type formatter. Consider the following controller:

```
public class AuthorsController : ApiController
{
    // ...

    public IQueryable<Author> Get()
    {
        return _repository.GetAll();
    }


    public Author Get(int id)
    {
        return _repository.Get(id);
    }
}
```

It is a simple controller with two methods to get a list or a single author. The author class is something like this:

```
public class Author
{
    public int Id { get; set; }
    public string Name { get; set; }
    public string PhotoUrl { get; set; }
}
```

So if we request a single author, we see:

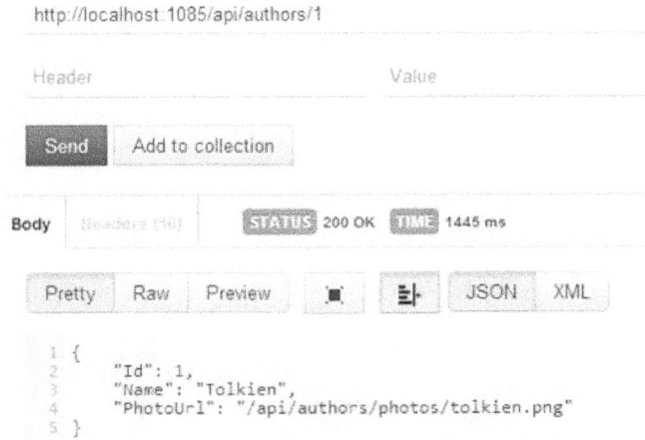

Figure 11: Getting a single author

What we want now is the photo of the author, but we would like to use the same URI we used to obtain the author info (`/api/authors/1`).

Therefore, we create a new GET request with the Accept header that specifies which format we want (for example, image/png).

Figure 12: A get request that specifies the accept type

As a response, we want a PNG image that represents Tolkien (the author with id 1).

To obtain this we need the help of a MediaTypeFormatter that takes the Author object from the controller and replaces it with his photo.

This is the complete implementation:

```
public class ImageFormatter : MediaTypeFormatter
{

    public ImageFormatter()

    {

        SupportedMediaTypes.Add(new MediaTypeHeaderValue("image/png"));
```

```
    }


    public override bool CanReadType(Type type)

    {

        return false;

    }


    public override bool CanWriteType(Type type)

    {

        return type == typeof(Author);

    }


    public override Task WriteToStreamAsync(Type type, object value, Stream writeStream, HttpContent content, TransportContext transportContext)

    {

        return Task.Factory.StartNew(() => WriteToStream(type, value, writeStream, content));

    }


    public void WriteToStream(Type type, object value, Stream stream, HttpContent content)

    {

        Author author = (Author)value;

        Image image = Image.FromFile(@".\Photos\" + author.Name + ".png");

        image.Save(stream, ImageFormat.Png);

        image.Dispose();

    }

}
```

This class inherits from MediaTypeFormatter, a base class for all the formatters. The runtime calls the WriteToStreamAsync, as noted previously. In this method, since it is asynchronous, we create a new Task and start it with the methods that actually read a file from the file system and write it to the output stream.

To add the newly created ImageFormatter media type formatter to the Web API pipeline, we need to register it by using the Formatters property on the HttpConfiguration object when the application starts:

```
public static class WebApiConfig

{

    public static void Register(HttpConfiguration config)
```

```
{
    config.Formatters.Add(new ImageFormatter());
}
}
```

The result when invoking the service is as follows:

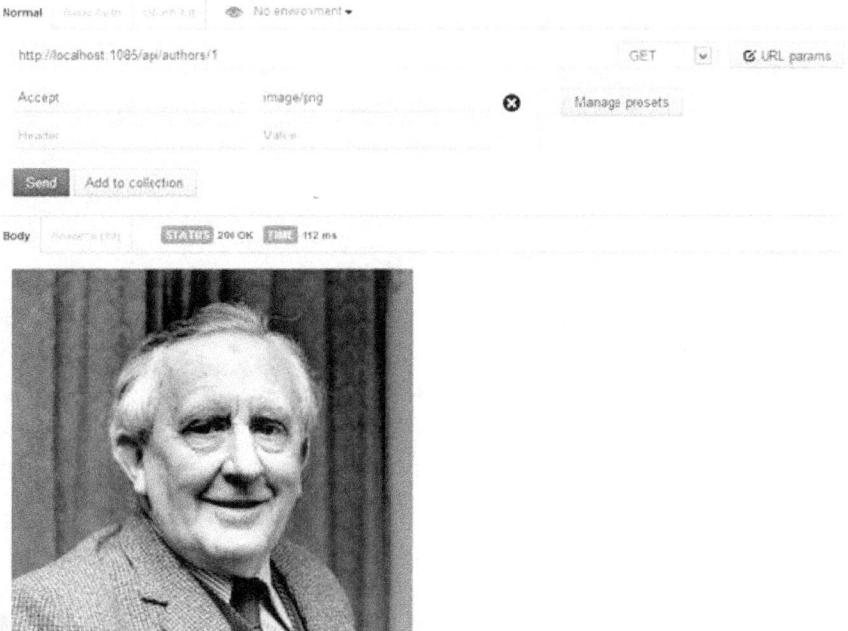

Figure 13: The response in PNG format

The nice thing is that with the same URI (remember that the URI represents the ID of a resource), we have two different representations, and we can decide which one we want using different headers.

Summary

Content negotiation is an important part of a real REST API. It makes it possible to expose a resource in various formats and let the client decide which is best. We saw how to implement a custom formatter to transform a resource in a PNG format so that the image representation of the resource could be provided to the client.

Chapter 8 Message Handlers

Onion architecture

We mentioned message handlers in Chapter 3 when we saw how a request is processed. Now we go a little deeper to understand how they are implemented and how they add functionality to our application.

The typical behavior of a message handler is to obtain the request, make some operation on the request, and then pass it to the next handler in the chain.

A message handler is simply a class that inherits the `HttpMessageHandler` abstract class. The interface of this class, if we take away the `IDisposable` interface, is only one method that receives the `HttpRequestMessage` and returns an `HttpResponseMessage`.

In fact, the aim of a message handler is simply to receive a request message (`HttpRequestMessage`) and return a response (`HttpResponseMessage`). The ASP.NET Web API composes these handlers in a chain where every handler is a reference to the next (through the `InnerHandler` property) so that a handler can execute the call and pass the result to the next. The final result is like an onion that is being traversed by the request and response messages.

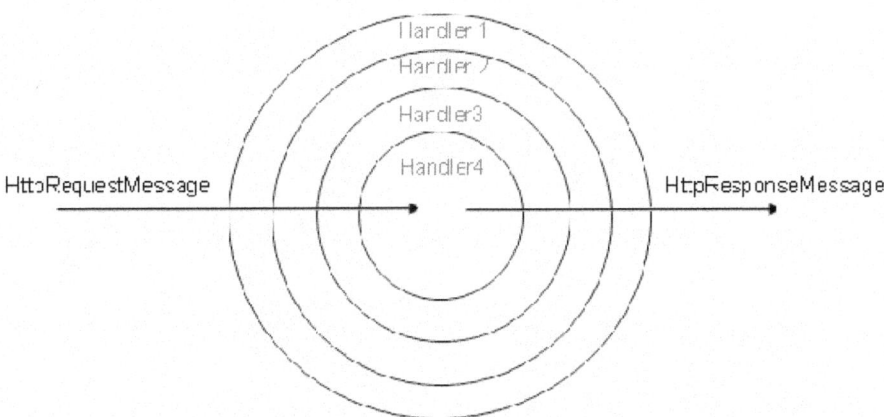

Message handlers can be used in several ways. For example, we could build a message handler that adds a custom header to the response. The code is very simple and reflects the simplicity in the architecture:

```
public class CustomHeaderMessageHandler : DelegatingHandler
{

    protected override Task<HttpResponseMessage> SendAsync
```

```
                      (
                          HttpRequestMessage request,

                          CancellationToken cancellationToken

                      )

    {

          request.Headers.Add("X-My-custom-Header", "this is a custom header");

          return base.SendAsync(request, cancellationToken);

    }

}
```

The previous code demonstrates how to create a handler that simply adds a new entry in the request header (x-My-custom-Header) and passes the call to the base class for further processing.

We are inheriting from the DelegatingHandler class that has already implemented the mechanism to manage the passing calls to the other handlers in the chain. DelegatingHandler itself derives from HttpMessageHandler.

Handlers could also be used to log the requests or the errors:

```
public class LogMessageHandler : DelegatingHandler

{

    protected override async Task<HttpResponseMessage> SendAsync

                      (

                          HttpRequestMessage request,

                          CancellationToken cancellationToken

                      )

    {

          HttpResponseMessage response = await base.SendAsync(request,

                                                    cancellationToken);

          if (!response.IsSuccessStatusCode)

          {

              // Log the error.

          }

          return response;

    }

}
```

In this case, we pass the call to the base class for execution since we need to know if the call was successful or an error was thrown. We get the response and write to the log in case of an error.

Once defined, a handler needs to be added to the configuration so that the ASP.NET Web API can use it in the execution pipeline:

```
// in WebApiConfig.cs

config.MessageHandlers.Add(new CustomHeaderMessageHandler());

config.MessageHandlers.Add(new LogMessageHandler());
```

We must consider that the order in which we register the handler is important, since it is executed in a top-down fashion. That is, the first entry is invoked first for a request message but last for a response message (as explained in the previous illustration).

Message handlers could also be registered per route instead of being applied globally. Registering a handler per route means that the handler takes place only for some requests:

```
IHttpRoute route = config.Routes.CreateRoute(

    routeTemplate: "api/Posts/{id}",

    defaults: new HttpRouteValueDictionary("route"),

    constraints: null,

    dataTokens: null,

    handler: new CustomHeaderMessageHandler());

config.Routes.Add("WithHandler", route);
```

In this case, we are using the `CustomHeaderMessageHandler` only for the `PostsController` as shown in the route template.

Summary

Handlers play a central part in the architecture of the ASP.NET Web API. The ability to modify the request and the response outside the service opens interesting scenarios and gives the possibility to extend the default framework's behavior.

In this chapter we looked at some basic background information about handlers and how to implement some custom handlers for specific circumstances.

Chapter 9 Security

Even if our APIs are public, we almost surely need some mechanism to check who is using our application.

There are two aspects of security to consider: authentication and authorization.

Authentication is the process that identifies who is the user that is using our API. Generally, authentication is implemented by using a username and password, a personal token, or, in complex cases, an OpenID provider.

Since one of the REST service constraints is that it must be stateless, the server should never store the client context between requests (the server should not use Session variables or a similar mechanism). Therefore, the client is forced to provide the credentials on every request.

This also means that the credentials are passed to the server in an HTTP header, and to make the requests secure we need to use a secure transport like HTTPS. Using HTTPS is at the base of every REST API that needs to be secured.

Authorization is the function of specifying if the user has the permission (access rights) to perform a specific task on a resource. Once the user is authenticated, the framework has to know if the user can view the requested data or save the information that is being posted.

There are various ways to authenticate a user, from a simple username and password, to a more sophisticated token, to OpenID.

With the ASP.NET Web API we can choose which one we prefer, but we have to implement it since nothing is ready out-of-the-box.

Let us start with the basic authentication that we need in most cases.

Basic Authentication

The first and simpler way to secure our API is to implement basic authentication. Basic authentication is a standard defined in RFC 2617. With this schema, the client must provide credentials to the server, which verifies the match. The credentials, username, and password are sent to the server using the `Authorization` header, and they are prefixed with the keyword `Basic` and encoded in Base64.

Username and password should be in the format of `username:password`, using the colon as separator.

For example, a request using the basic authentication looks something like this:

```
GET http://localhost:1085/api/Values HTTP/1.1

Host: localhost:1085

Proxy-Connection: keep-alive

User-Agent: Mozilla/5.0 (Windows NT 6.2; WOW64) AppleWebKit/537.31 (KHTML, like Gecko) Chrome/26
.0.1410.43 Safari/537.31

Cache-Control: no-cache

Authorization: Basic ZW1hOnB3ZA==

Accept: */*

Accept-Encoding: gzip,deflate,sdch

Accept-Language: en-US,en;q=0.8,it;q=0.6

Accept-Charset: ISO-8859-1,utf-8;q=0.7,*;q=0.3
```

In bold we can see the `Authorization` header with the username and password that are encoded in Base64.

The server then receives the request and extracts the `Authorization` header to validate the credentials. It decodes the string and verifies whether the username and password are correct. If they are correct, it continues with the execution of the request. Otherwise, it returns an `HTTP 401 Unauthorized` response. In this example, the response contains the header `WWW-Authenticate: Basic` that instructs the client to provide the correct credentials using the Basic scheme. This header is the one that browsers use to show the username and password dialog box to the user.

That's how the basic authentication works. Let us now see what this means to our ASP.NET Web API application.

To manage the authentication request, we need to implement a `Message Handler` that receives the request before it arrives to the controller and decides if the user has the rights to access the resource.

To implement a `MessageHandler` we have to implement the `DelegatingHandler` abstract class as we have already seen in previous chapters.

```csharp
public class BasicAuthenticationHandler : DelegatingHandler
{
    private readonly IAuthenticationService _service;

    public BasicAuthenticationHandler(IAuthenticationService service)
    {
        _service = service;
    }

    protected override Task<HttpResponseMessage> SendAsync(
                            HttpRequestMessage request,
                            CancellationToken cancellationToken)
    {
        AuthenticationHeaderValue authHeader = request.Headers.Authorization;
        if (authHeader == null || authHeader.Scheme != "Basic")
        {
            return Unauthorized(request);
        }

        string encodedCredentials = authHeader.Parameter;
        byte[] credentialBytes = Convert.FromBase64String(encodedCredentials);
        string[] credentials = Encoding.ASCII
                            .GetString(credentialBytes).Split(':');

        if (!_service.Authenticate(credentials[0], credentials[1]))
        {
            return Unauthorized(request);
        }

        string[] roles = null; // TODO
        IIdentity identity = new GenericIdentity(credentials[0], "Basic");
        IPrincipal user = new GenericPrincipal(identity, roles);
        HttpContext.Current.User = user;
```

```
        return base.SendAsync(request, cancellationToken);

    }


    private Task<HttpResponseMessage> Unauthorized(HttpRequestMessage request)

    {

        var response = request.CreateResponse(HttpStatusCode.Unauthorized);

        response.Headers.Add("WWW-Authenticate", "Basic");


        TaskCompletionSource<HttpResponseMessage> task = new TaskCompletionSource<HttpResponseMessage>();

        task.SetResult(response);

        return task.Task;

    }

}
```

Let's see what happens. When a request arrives to the handler, it analyzes the header by searching for the Authentication value. If it is not present, it sends a 401 Unauthorized message to the client.

If the Authentication header is present, it decodes its value from Base64 and extracts the value of the username and password:

```
AuthenticationHeaderValue authHeader = request.Headers.Authorization;

if (authHeader == null || authHeader.Scheme != "Basic")

{

    return Unauthorized(request);

}


string encodedCredentials = authHeader.Parameter;

byte[] credentialBytes = Convert.FromBase64String(encodedCredentials);

string[] credentials = Encoding.ASCII.GetString(credentialBytes).split(':');
```

Now in credentials we have the two strings, username and password. We can now use a service (something that uses a database or other storage) to verify if the credentials are correct:

```
if (!_service.Authenticate(credentials[0], credentials[1]))

{

    return Unauthorized(request);

}
```

The `IAuthenticationService.Authenticate` method is implemented as follows:

```
public interface IAuthenticationService
{
    bool Authenticate(string user, string password);
}


public class AuthenticationService: IAuthenticationService
{
    public bool Authenticate(string user, string password)
    {
        //Do database calls and check if
        //the user and password matches.
        return true;
    }
}
```

If the service responds true, that means the user can access the resource, and if not, it sends an `Unauthorized` message to the client. The last part of the method is meant to build the `Principal` and `Identity` information that needs to be used in conjunction with the ASP.NET membership.

```
string[] roles = null; // TODO
IIdentity identity = new GenericIdentity(credentials[0], "Basic");
IPrincipal user = new GenericPrincipal(identity, roles);
HttpContext.Current.User = user;


return base.SendAsync(request, cancellationToken);
```

The part that generates the `Unauthorized` response is quite simple:

```
private Task<HttpResponseMessage> Unauthorized(HttpRequestMessage request)
{
    var response = request.CreateResponse(HttpStatusCode.Unauthorized);
    response.Headers.Add("WWW-Authenticate", "Basic");

    var task = new TaskCompletionSource<HttpResponseMessage>();
    task.SetResult(response);
    return task.Task;
}
```

It simply builds the correct `HttpResponseMessage` with the status code `401 Unauthorized` and adds the header `WWW-Authenticate: basic` to ask the client for the credentials.

Once implemented, this handler must be registered in the API configuration:

```
GlobalConfiguration.Configuration.MessageHandlers.Add(new BasicAuthenticationHandler(new Authent
icationService()));
```

This can be done in the `WebApiConfig` class. It simply adds the handler to the collection of already configured handlers.

Now that everything is wired up we can try to call our API using Postman:

Figure 14: Calling a secure API without providing username and password

If we don't provide the header, the server responds with a `401 Unauthorized` status, but if we add the header with correct credentials, the server returns the requested resource.

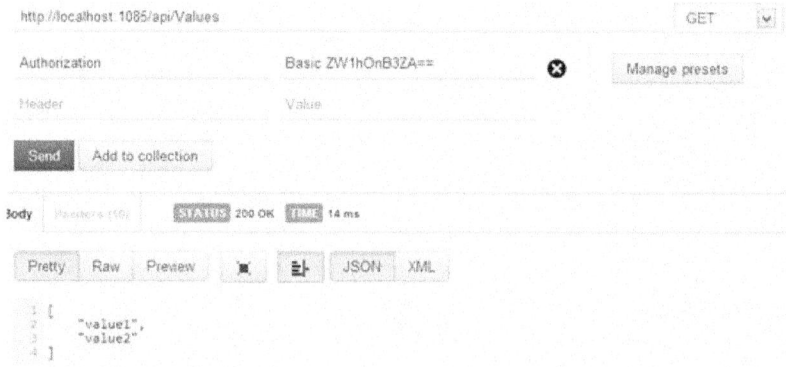

Figure 15: Issuing a request with basic authentication

Since basic authentication puts the credential in the header in clear text (even if it is encoded in Base64), we need to expose the API using a secure protocol like HTTPS.

Token Authentication

Token authentication is not a standard model even though it is widely used in the API implementation. Often the client is not a user but another application, in which case username and password are not relevant. In these cases, the API provider gives a token to the application that needs access. Depending on implementation, this token may or may not have a due date. Technically this process works the same way basic authentication does; it is based on the header `Authorization` and generally uses another schema (instead of Basic).

In reality, since there is not a standard, other custom headers could be used as well. The token in the header could be encrypted with a private/public key pair to obtain better security levels.

OpenID and OAuth

OpenID and OAuth are two different methods for managing application security.

OpenID is an open, decentralized, free framework for user-centric digital identity. It takes advantage of already existing internet technology and recognizes that people are already creating identities for themselves, whether through their blog, photo stream, profile page, etc. With OpenID we can easily transform one of these existing URIs into an account which can be used at sites that support OpenID logins. In this case, the OpenID provider authenticates the user and passes a credential token to the API that needs to know the identity of the user. To better understand how OpenID works, take a look at the foundation site at http://openid.net/, especially the "Getting Started" section.

OAuth is a little bit different in that it's not meant to authenticate the user but to let the API act as if it is the user. With OAuth, the application can call other applications on the user's behalf so that the calling applications are not obliged to store the user credentials.

The applications we can access using OAuth authentication can also revoke the permission.

More information on OAuth can be found on the site http://oauth.net/.

 Note: ASP.NET Web API doesn't have built-in support for OpenID and OAuth, so it's up to us to implement them. Fortunately there are various NuGet packages that add support to our API. One of them is DotNetOpenAuth (http://www.dotnetopenauth.net/).

Summary

Security is a complex topic, and a single chapter is too short to be exhaustive. We just examined two basic techniques to secure our API, basic authentication and token authentication. Both are based on a custom message handler that requests to extract the header that contains security information.

Chapter 10 OData

OData Basics

Open Data Protocol is a web protocol designed by Microsoft with the aim to create a new protocol for querying and updating data over HTTP. OData is an Open protocol, which means that various implementation methods are available for it.

ASP.NET Web API has built-in support for OData so that you can query your resources using the HTTP protocol and the OData syntax. Complete support for Web API was added with the Visual Studio 2012 Update 2, or with the Microsoft ASP.NET Web API OData NuGet package.

We will now build a simple API with OData support.

Consider this controller:

```
public class PostsController : EntitySetController<Post,int>
{

    private readonly IPostRepository _repository;


    public PostsController(IPostRepository repository)
    {

        _repository = repository;

    }


    public override IQueryable<Post> Get()
    {

        IEnumerable<Post> posts= _repository.GetPosts();

        return posts.AsQueryable();

    }

}
```

This controller does not inherit from the usual `ApiController`, but instead is an `EntitySetController`. `EntitySetController` is an abstract class that inherits from `ODataController`, which inherits from `ApiController`.

The complete hierarchy is:

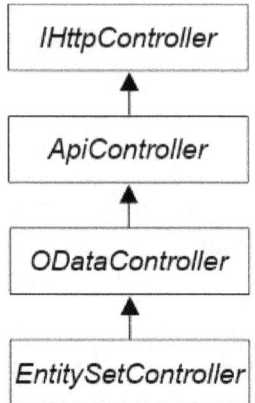

Figure 16: EntitySetController hierarchy

The `EntitySetController` is just a specialized `ApiController` that has built-in facilities to manage the OData requests and to build OData responses.

In the previous example, the controller is declared as `EntitySetController<Post, int>`. The two generic parameters represent the entity type exposed by this endpoint and the type of the entity Id. So the post class could be something like this:

```
public class Post
{
    public int Id { get; set; }

    public string Title { get; set; }

    public string Author { get; set; }

    public DateTime PublishingDate { get; set; }
}
```

Then we override the `Get` method of `EntitySetController` and implement it so that it returns the list as `IQueryable<Post>`. The `IQueryable` is needed by the OData controller, which uses it to add the query that is eventually provided in the `GET` request.

This is not enough to make the OData protocol work with the Web API; we need some more configuration. In the `WebApiConfig` class, we have to add this code:

```
ODataModelBuilder modelBuilder = new ODataConventionModelBuilder();

modelBuilder.EntitySet<Post>("Posts");


Microsoft.Data.Edm.IEdmModel model = modelBuilder.GetEdmModel();

config.Routes.MapODataRoute("ODataRoute", "odata", model);


config.EnableQuerySupport();
```

This code creates and configures the OData endpoint and defines a new route for the OData requests. Please note that the new route won't use the /api route, but instead will start with odata, as defined in the MapODataRoute. Another thing to note is that the URI in the previous case will be case sensitive, so the correct URI would become /odata/Posts.

The EnableQuerySupport command is necessary if we want to enable the query protocol of OData.

Now we are ready to launch the application and test the OData protocol:

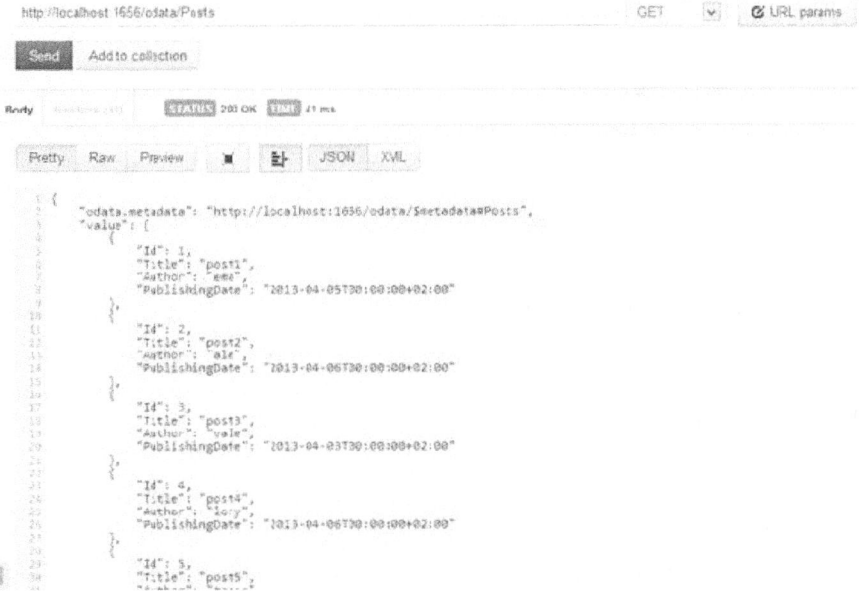

Figure 17: A simple get to an OData Endpoint

The result is not so different from the one with the default ApiController. The only real difference is in the attribute odata.metadata that specifies a URL to which we can ask information about the Post resource. If we invoke that URI, we obtain:

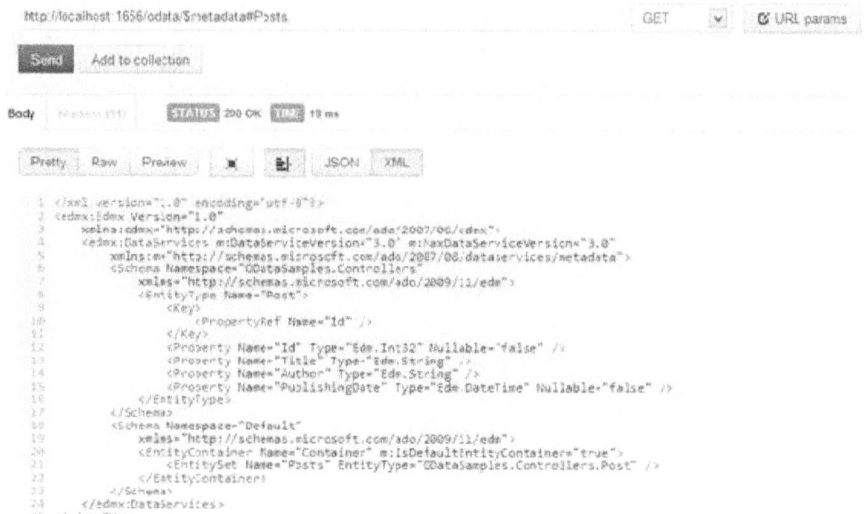

Figure 18: Resource metadata

This XML describes the Post resource showing properties and its types other than general information about the entity.

However, the real power of OData is in the fact that you can generate requests using a special syntax that enables you to create complex queries to filter, order, and aggregate the results.

Let's start by adding an order by clause to the URI:

`/odata/Posts?$orderby=PublishingDate`

The orderby option instructs the OData engine that we want the result ordered by publishing date. We do not have to modify the code, since the OData modules of the ASP.NET Web API parse the Query String and the filters are applied to the IQueryable result.

The currently supported options are: top, orderby, filter, inlinecount, and skip.

Orderby

orderby is used to specify how the result must be sorted. The default sorting is in ascending order, but we can specify the type of sort using this syntax:

`/odata/Posts?$orderby=Author desc`

We can also combine different attributes:

`/odata/Posts?$orderby=Author,PublishingDate`

Top

```
/odata/Posts?$top=2
```

`top` is used to specify the number of items to return. With `$top=2`, we are saying that we want just two elements.

Filter

```
/odata/Posts?$filter=Author%20eq%20'ema'
```

`filter` is used to restrict the result (like the "where" clause in SQL). In the this example, we requested the posts of the author "ema."

`filter` can also be used with Boolean and comparison operators.

Table 7: OData Boolean operators

Operator	Description	C# equivalent
eq	Equal	==
ne	Not equal	!=
gt	Greater than	>
ge	Greater than or equal	>=
lt	Less than	<
le	Less than or equal	<=
and	And	&&
or	Or	||

With these operators, we can create more complex queries:

```
/odata/Posts?$filter=Author%20eq%20'ema'%20and%20Title%20eq%20'post2'
```

```
/odata/Posts?$filter=Author%20eq%20'ema'%20or%20Author%20eq%20'tessa'
```

Inlinecount

`inlinecount` is used to add information about the number of items in the collection:

```
/odata/Posts?$inlinecount=allpages
```

The `allpages` value is defined in the OData specification and MUST include a count of the number of entities in the collection identified by the URI (after applying any `$filter` system query options present on the URI).

Skip

`skip` is used to skip the first *n* values and return only the next:

```
/odata/Posts?$skip=2
```

In this example, `skip` returns only the elements starting from the third element in the list.

OData is capable of much more than this; the protocol also specifies the way to modify resources, but the details are beyond the scope of this book.

Summary

OData is an interesting technology that can be used to query our API. Instead of creating many endpoints with various parameters to match the entire possible request, an OData endpoint resolves most of the problems in just a few lines of code. In this chapter, we saw how it works and the basic syntax used to build the queries.

Chapter 11 Hosting

Now that we have built our Web API application, it needs to be hosted. The first option we have is called web-host. It uses Internet Information Server (IIS), like the ASP.NET MVC application. We don't go into the details of this kind of hosting in this book because it is the well-known way to host web applications in the Microsoft ecosystem.

Self-hosting

The other option, self-hosting, is a new way to host web applications. Practically, this means implementing a console application (or a Windows service, or any other runnable application) that is the host for our API.

The code is quite simple: all we have to do is to create a new console application, add a reference to the `Microsoft.AspNet.WebApi.SelfHost` package using NuGet, and write the following code in `Main()`:

```
static void Main()
{

    var config = new HttpSelfHostConfiguration("http://localhost:3000");


    config.Routes.MapHttpRoute("default",

                        "api/{controller}/{id}",

                            new { id = RouteParameter.Optional });


    var server = new HttpSelfHostServer(config);

    server.OpenAsync().Wait();

    Console.ReadLine();

}
```

What we have done here is create a new configuration and define the base URL at which the API will respond. We choose `localhost` and port `3000`.

On the configuration, we set the route map with the usual pattern (`api/controller/id`); we can add all the needed entries to this map as illustrated in Chapter 4.

Next, we create a new instance of `HttpSelfHostServer` with the new configuration, and lastly, we start the server and wait for incoming requests.

Now we can compile and run the application, and test it with our client:

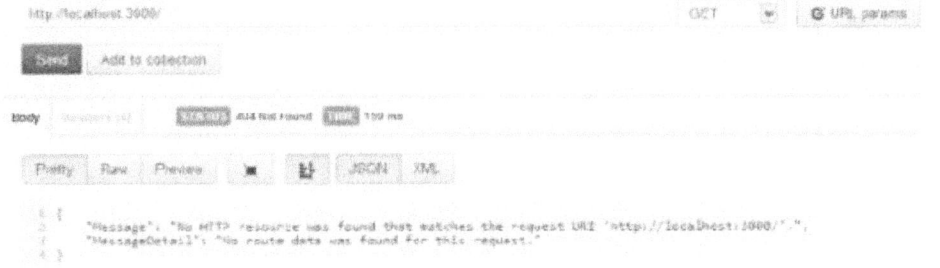

Figure 19: A call to a misconfigured self-host application

```
No HTTP resource was found that matches the request URI 'http://localhost:3000/'.
```

What we get is an error that makes perfect sense, since we have not created any controller yet.

What we can do now is add an `ApiControllers` implementation to make something useful with our application. This means that the application doesn't have to be a Web API application template; a console application could also become a host.

We add a simple controller:

```
public class HelloController : ApiController
{
    public string[] Get()
    {
        return new[]{"Wow", "this", "is", "a", "real", "web", "app"};
    }
}
```

With this controller implemented, we can re-run the console application and call it from the client:

Figure 20: A call to a self-host controller

What we have is a real ASP.NET Web API application that does not need a full web server like IIS. This is very useful for exposing the API through a Windows service, for example, or for installing the API to a PC that does not have IIS installed.

If we want to use an existing Web API project and host it in the self-host mode, we just need to reference the project and change the code in the `WebApiConfig` class to use the `HttpConfiguration` that the console application has created.

In-memory hosting

The last option to hosting a Web API application is to use the in-memory host. It is called in-memory because there are not any real HTTP remote connections between the client and the server but the client (usually an HttpClient) is directly connected to the HttpServer instance.

Since the HttpServer class inherits from HttpMessageHandler, it can be used to create an instance of HttpClient class so that the two instances are directly connected.

This kind of configuration is not useful in a real world scenario, but it is perfect for testing, as we will see in the next chapter. Since the client and the server are in the same process and they are connected in memory, the performance of the communication is very high, and our test executes quickly.

For in-memory hosting, the code is very similar to the self-hosting option:

```
public static void Main()
{
    var config = new HttpConfiguration();
    config.Routes.MapHttpRoute("default",
                        "api/{controller}/{id}",
                        new { id = RouteParameter.Optional });

    HttpServer server = new HttpServer(config);

    HttpClient client = new HttpClient(server);

    var response = client.GetAsync("http://localhost/api/hello").Result;
    String content = response.Content.ReadAsStringAsync().Result;
}
```

The previous code is taken from a console application. We create the configuration as usual, and we create an instance of HttpServer (in the self-hosting scenario we used the HttpSelfHostingServer).

Next we create an HttpClient to issue a request. The HttpClient needs in its constructor an instance of HttpMessageHandler, and like we already said, HttpServer implements that class, so it fits perfectly.

With the client, we can build a request using the GetAsync method and specifying the URI. The result is an HttpResponseMessage from which we get the content, and, in the content, we will have the result in a string format.

The fact that client and server are so tightly coupled help us in writing an integration test to verify that our API works as expected.

Summary

Hosting is an important topic and the new self-host scenario opens new possibilities for distributing our Web API application. The fact that a Windows service could become an HTTP endpoint is helpful in all cases in which we need to expose a behavior for other applications. Outside of these cases, we don't need to have a full web server like Internet Information Server to host our API, and the deployment becomes an xcopy installation.

Chapter 12 Testing

Like ASP.NET MVC, ASP.NET Web API was written with testability in mind. This means that we can develop REST services using test-driven development, or just add unit tests or integration tests to our existing applications. If we take a look at the ASP.NET source code, the main solution contains more than 1,000 tests—Microsoft is serious about testing.

One of the pillars of testability is the decoupling of the elements that are being tested. In our case this means that the controllers should be decoupled from other components. We can only write test units with decoupled controllers; if we can't get the complete decoupling, we can write only integration tests.

Consider the following controller with just three actions:

```
public class PostsController : ApiController

{

    private readonly PostRepository _repository;


    public PostsController()

    {

        _repository = new PostRepository();

    }


    public IQueryable<Post> Get()

    {

        return _repository.GetAll();

    }


    public Post Get(int id)

    {

        return _repository.Get(id);

    }


    public HttpResponseMessage Post(Post post)

    {

        _repository.Create(post);

        var response = Request.CreateResponse(HttpStatusCode.Created);
```

```
        string uri = Url.Link("DefaultApi", new { id = post.Id });
        response.Headers.Location = new Uri(uri);


        return response;

    }

}
```

How can we unit test this controller?

It's impossible since it has a strong dependency on the repository class and since the controller creates the instance of the repository inside the constructor. The new operation is what really couples the PostController with the PostRepository. So if we would like to test the controller, we have to deal with the complete stack and running an integration test rather than a unit test.

Unit tests vs. integration tests

Unit and integration are just two different types of tests with different purposes. Unit tests are built to test a single method in isolation from the rest of the application. This means that the test and the system under test (SUT) must not use external resources (database, file system, networks, etc.) and that the tested code must not depend on other objects. In integration tests, we are writing a test against the complete stack of our application, which means that the class under test is connected to other real classes that can use databases or other external resources.

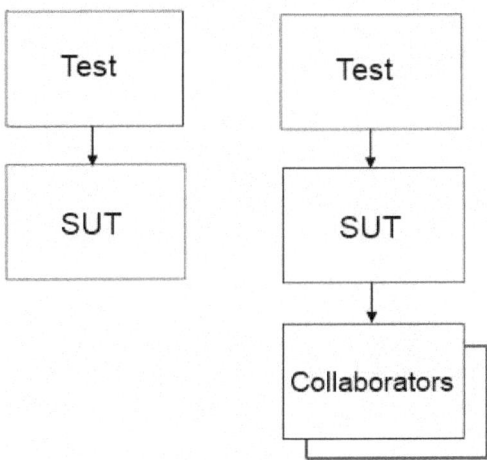

Figure 21: Unit tests vs. integration tests

What does this mean practically?

Unit tests are usually faster because they are executed completely in memory, while integration tests tend to be slower, since they could depend on external resources. If a unit test breaks, the error is quite certainly in the method that we are testing, but if an integration test breaks, the error could be in other parts of the application, and sometimes it might not be a "real" error (for example, if the connection string is not correct, or if the database server is unreachable).

So are unit tests better than integration tests? Absolutely not—every test is important. Unit tests are designed for micro functionality, while integration tests verify the application in its completeness.

Decoupling the controller with dependency injection

Going back to our `PostsController`, let's see how we can refactor it to support better testability. We have already said that the problem is in the constructor that creates an instance of the repository. If we can apply the dependency injection pattern and pass to the controller an abstraction of the repository, we can write unit tests.

So we can refactor the controller to make it receive an instance of the interface `IPostRepository`:

```
public class PostsController : ApiController
{

    private readonly IPostRepository _repository;


    public PostsController(IPostRepository repository)

    {

        _repository = repository;

    }



    //...

}
```

This refactoring allows us to unit test the `PostsController` because we remove the strong dependency. In our test we can pass a mocked repository:

```
[Fact]
public void GetById_should_return_the_post()

{

    Mock<IPostRepository> repo = new Mock<IPostRepository>();

    PostsController controller = new PostsController(repo.Object);


    controller.Get(42);


    repo.Verify(r => r.Get(42));

}
```

We have created a mock instance of the repository and created the controller. We can verify that when we call `Get` on the controller, the repository is called with the right parameters. Since the repository is a mock object and the controller is not using the real repository, this is a unit test.

State testing vs. interaction testing

Using mock objects, we can write two different styles of unit tests. **State-based testing** checks the correctness of the SUT, verifying the state of the SUT after the execution of the tested method.
Interaction-based testing checks the correctness of the implementation, verifying that the SUT makes the correct calls to the collaborators so that it doesn't need to verify the state of the SUT. In this example we have written an interaction test.

But this refactoring breaks our application; even if the test is green, if we run the application and call the `Get` from the client, we obtain the following error:

```
Type 'HelloWebApi.Controllers.PostsController' does not have a default constructor"
```

What happens here is that since Web API is not capable of building a controller that has external dependencies, it searches for the default constructor. Since it does not find it, it throws an exception.

To resolve this problem we have to implement a custom controller resolver that is able to resolve the dependencies and construct the controller.

Practically, this means we implement the interface `IDependencyResolver` and change the default resolver to the new one. The interface `IDependencyResolver` (which implements `IDependencyScope` and `IDisposable`) provides two methods:

- `GetService`: Used to obtain an instance of a single component of the specified type.
- `GetServices`: Used to obtain a collection of objects of the specified type.

So for the controllers, the runtime calls `GetService`. If our custom controller is able to create the required type, it builds it and returns it. If not, it simply returns null so that the runtime continues with the default resolver.

The custom controller can also manage the lifetime of the objects that it creates; the two methods `BeginScope` and `Dispose` are used for this. When the framework creates a new instance of a controller, it calls `BeginScope`, which returns an instance of `IDependencyScope`. Then, the runtime calls `GetService` on the `IDependencyScope` instance to get the controller instance. When the request is completed, the runtime calls `Dispose` on the child scope, so we can use `Dispose` to dispose of the controller's dependencies.

Therefore, in practice, a simple resolver could be something like this:

```
public class SimpleResolver : IDependencyResolver
{
    public object GetService(Type serviceType)
    {
        if (serviceType == typeof(PostsController))
```

```
    {

        return new PostsController(new PostRepository());

    }

    return null;

}


public IEnumerable<object> GetServices(Type serviceType)

{

    return new List<object>();

}


public void Dispose()

{

}


public IDependencyScope BeginScope()

{

    return this;

}

}
```

The most important part is in the GetService method that is in charge of building the requested object based on serviceType. In the previous implementation, we just created the PostsController using the new operator. In a real world scenario, that code should probably be replaced with an inversion of control container that will resolve the object for us.

Now that we have the resolver correctly implemented, we need to add it to the configuration to make sure it works. Add this line to the WebApiConfig.Register method:

```
config.DependencyResolver = new SimpleResolver();
```

Unit testing a controller

Going back to the testing topic, let's see how we can test the `Post` action:

```csharp
public HttpResponseMessage Post(Post post)
{
    _repository.Create(post);

    var response = Request.CreateResponse(HttpStatusCode.Created);


    string uri = Url.Link("DefaultApi", new { id = post.Id });
    response.Headers.Location = new URI(uri);


    return response;
}
```

This action creates a new `Post` object using the controller, and then creates a response with the status code and sets the location header to the newly created post. We would like to test that the response message contains the correct status code and that the header is present.

Testing this code is easy, but requires a bit of setup for preparing the context for the request and response.

The complete code for the test is here:

```csharp
[Fact]
public void Post_Status_is_Created_and_header_contains_the_location()
{
    Mock<IPostRepository> repository = new Mock<IPostRepository>();


    var controller = new PostsController(repository.Object);


    var config = new HttpConfiguration();
    var request = new HttpRequestMessage(HttpMethod.Post,
                                "http://localhost/");

    IHttpRoute route = config.Routes.MapHttpRoute("DefaultApi",
                                "api/{controller}/{id}");

    HttpRouteData routeData = new HttpRouteData(route,
                                new HttpRouteValueDictionary
                                {
```

```
                                                        { "controller", "posts" }
                                            });

    controller.ControllerContext =

                        new HttpControllerContext(config, routeData, request);

    request.Properties[HttpPropertyKeys.HttpConfigurationKey] = config;

    request.Properties[HttpPropertyKeys.HttpRouteDataKey] = routeData;

    controller.Request = request;

    HttpResponseMessage response = controller.Post(new Post() {

        Title = "test",

        Date = DateTime.Today,

        Body = "blablabla"

    });

    Assert.Equal(HttpStatusCode.Created, response.StatusCode);

    Assert.NotNull(response.Headers.Location);

}
```

The test starts with the creation of the mock repository, which is needed to make the test pass, even if it's not used in the test. After the creation of the controller, all that code is needed to set up the context in which the Web API needs to run, so it can use the helper methods like `Request.CreateResponse` and `Url.Link`. Basically we create the route table, the request object, the configuration, and the `ControllerContext`.

 Note: The sample tests are written using xunit.net (http://xunit.codeplex.com/) as a test.

Next, we call the `Post()` method by passing a fake `Post` object. We `Assert` on the response message to make sure that the status code is correct and that the location header is present.

The POST action is the most difficult action to test. Others like GET and DELETE are much simpler because they don't have to deal with the request and response mechanism. Therefore, this test is not as beautiful as it should be because the setup code is hard to write and read. We could certainly refactor it, creating helper methods or abstract classes to inherit from, but we can also use a special hosting technique to test the controller in integration with the full ASP.NET Web API stack.

Integration test with in-memory hosting

We already talked about in-memory hosting in the previous chapter, and we have already shown how it works. Here we will see how we can use it to test our controllers. With in-memory hosting, we could write integration tests as if the ASP.NET Web API is in a production environment. So a test in this scenario passes the full stack, from the request down to the model binders, controllers, repositories, and back to the response. This is the perfect technique for writing acceptance tests on the behavior of the API.

```
[Fact]
public void Get_with_in_memory_hosting()
{

    HttpConfiguration config = new HttpConfiguration();

    WebApiConfig.Register(config);


    HttpServer server = new HttpServer(config);


    HttpClient client = new HttpClient(server);
    var response = client.GetAsync("http://localhost/api/posts").Result;


    Assert.Equal(HttpStatusCode.OK, response.StatusCode);

}
```

This test is simpler than the previous one; it creates an in-memory server that "listens" to the requests that are issued using the HttpClient class that it asserts against the response. This is an integration test since it uses the entire application stack. As you can see at the beginning of the test, we have to configure the API using the WebApiConfig class so that the test configuration is the same as it would be in production. The thing to notice is that even if we are testing the PostsController in the test, it is not directly used. Instead, we build a request to the /api/posts URI, the routing system that routes the request to the PostsController (exactly how it happens in a production scenario).

The test for the Post() action is something like this:

```
[Fact]
public void Get_with_in_memory_hosting()
{

    HttpConfiguration config = new HttpConfiguration();

    WebApiConfig.Register(config);
```

```
HttpServer server = new HttpServer(config);


HttpClient client = new HttpClient(server);

HashSet<KeyValuePair<string, string>> values = new

    HashSet<KeyValuePair<string, string>>{

        new KeyValuePair<string, string>("Title", "test"),

        new KeyValuePair<string, string>("Date", "2010-04-11"),

        new KeyValuePair<string, string>("Body", "blablabla")

    };

HttpResponseMessage response = client.PostAsync("http://localhost/api/posts", new FormUrlEnc
odedContent(values)).Result;


Assert.Equal(HttpStatusCode.Created, response.StatusCode);

Assert.NotNull(response.Headers.Location);

}
```

We do not need to set up the entire context in this case since it is automatically configured by the in-memory server. What we have to do is build the request. Since this is a POST, the request must have a body. We are using a FormUrlEncodedContent, which is a HashSet with the key-value pairs that represent the information about the Post to be created.

Summary

Testing is often considered an accessory to the real application, perhaps because in the past, testing web applications was very difficult. ASP.NET Web API makes testing as easy as writing other parts of the application. And since test-driven development is applicable, our API grows test after test.

In this chapter, we saw how to test Web API, and how to apply inversion of control to inject dependencies so that the tests created are real unit tests.

Appendix A: HTTP Status Codes (RFC 2616)

Informational 1xx

This class of status code indicates a provisional response, consisting only of the Status-Line and optional headers, and is terminated by an empty line. There are no required headers for this class of status code. Since HTTP/1.0 did not define any 1xx status codes, servers MUST NOT send a 1xx response to an HTTP/1.0 client except under experimental conditions.

A client MUST be prepared to accept one or more 1xx status responses prior to a regular response, even if the client does not expect a 100 (Continue) status message. Unexpected 1xx status responses MAY be ignored by a user agent.

Proxies MUST forward 1xx responses, unless the connection between the proxy and its client has been closed, or unless the proxy itself requested the generation of the 1xx response. (For example, if a proxy adds an "Expect: 100-continue" field when it forwards a request, then it need not forward the corresponding 100 (Continue) response(s).)

100 Continue

The client SHOULD continue with its request. This interim response is used to inform the client that the initial part of the request has been received and has not yet been rejected by the server. The client SHOULD continue by sending the remainder of the request or, if the request has already been completed, ignore this response. The server MUST send a final response after the request has been completed.

101 Switching Protocols

The server understands and is willing to comply with the client's request, via the Upgrade message header field, for a change in the application protocol being used on this connection. The server will switch protocols to those defined by the response's Upgrade header field immediately after the empty line which terminates the 101 response.

The protocol SHOULD be switched only when it is advantageous to do so. For example, switching to a newer version of HTTP is advantageous over older versions, and switching to a real-time, synchronous protocol might be advantageous when delivering resources that use such features.

Successful 2xx

This class of status code indicates that the client's request was successfully received, understood, and accepted.

200 OK

The request has succeeded. The information returned with the response is dependent on the method used in the request, for example:

GET an entity corresponding to the requested resource is sent in the response;

HEAD the entity-header fields corresponding to the requested resource are sent in the response without any message-body;

POST an entity describing or containing the result of the action;

TRACE an entity containing the request message as received by the end server.

201 Created

The request has been fulfilled and resulted in a new resource being created. The newly created resource can be referenced by the URI(s) returned in the entity of the response, with the most specific URI for the resource given by a Location header field. The response SHOULD include an entity containing a list of resource characteristics and location(s) from which the user or user agent can choose the one most appropriate. The entity format is specified by the media type given in the Content-Type header field. The origin server MUST create the resource before returning the 201 status code. If the action cannot be carried out immediately, the server SHOULD respond with 202 (Accepted) response instead.

A 201 response MAY contain an ETag response header field indicating the current value of the entity tag for the requested variant just created.

202 Accepted

The request has been accepted for processing, but the processing has not been completed. The request might or might not eventually be acted upon, as it might be disallowed when processing actually takes place. There is no facility for re-sending a status code from an asynchronous operation such as this.

The 202 response is intentionally non-committal. Its purpose is to allow a server to accept a request for some other process (perhaps a batch-oriented process that is only run once per day) without requiring that the user agent's connection to the server persist until the process is completed. The entity returned with this response SHOULD include an indication of the request's current status and either a pointer to a status monitor or some estimate of when the user can expect the request to be fulfilled.

203 Non-Authoritative Information

The returned metainformation in the entity-header is not the definitive set as available from the origin server, but is gathered from a local or a third-party copy. The set presented MAY be a subset or superset of the original version. For example, including local annotation information about the resource might result in a superset of the metainformation known by the origin server. Use of this response code is not required and is only appropriate when the response would otherwise be 200 (OK).

204 No Content

The server has fulfilled the request but does not need to return an entity-body, and might want to return updated metainformation. The response MAY include new or updated metainformation in the form of entity-headers, which if present SHOULD be associated with the requested variant.

If the client is a user agent, it SHOULD NOT change its document view from that which caused the request to be sent. This response is primarily intended to allow input for actions to take place without causing a change to the user agent's active document view, although any new or updated metainformation SHOULD be applied to the document currently in the user agent's active view.

The 204 response MUST NOT include a message-body, and thus is always terminated by the first empty line after the header fields.

205 Reset Content

The server has fulfilled the request and the user agent SHOULD reset the document view which caused the request to be sent. This response is primarily intended to allow input for actions to take place via user input, followed by a clearing of the form in which the input is given so that the user can easily initiate another input action. The response MUST NOT include an entity.

206 Partial Content

The server has fulfilled the partial GET request for the resource. The request MUST have included a Range header field indicating the desired range, and MAY have included an If-Range header field to make the request conditional.

If the 206 response is the result of an If-Range request that used a strong cache validator, the response SHOULD NOT include other entity-headers. If the response is the result of an If-Range request that used a weak validator, the response MUST NOT include other entity-headers; this prevents inconsistencies between cached entity-bodies and updated headers. Otherwise, the response MUST include all of the entity-headers that would have been returned with a 200 (OK) response to the same request.

A cache MUST NOT combine a 206 response with other previously cached content if the ETag or Last-Modified headers do not match exactly.

A cache that does not support the Range and Content-Range headers MUST NOT cache 206 (Partial) responses.

Redirection 3xx

This class of status code indicates that further action needs to be taken by the user agent in order to fulfill the request. The action required MAY be carried out by the user agent without interaction with the user if and only if the method used in the second request is GET or HEAD. A client SHOULD detect infinite redirection loops, since such loops generate network traffic for each redirection.

300 Multiple Choices

The requested resource corresponds to any one of a set of representations, each with its own specific location, and agent-driven negotiation information (section 12) is being provided so that the user (or user agent) can select a preferred representation and redirect its request to that location.

Unless it was a HEAD request, the response SHOULD include an entity containing a list of resource characteristics and location(s) from which the user or user agent can choose the one most appropriate. The entity format is specified by the media type given in the Content-Type header field. Depending upon the format and the capabilities of the user agent, selection of the most appropriate choice MAY be performed automatically. However, this specification does not define any standard for such automatic selection.

If the server has a preferred choice of representation, it SHOULD include the specific URI for that representation in the Location field; user agents MAY use the Location field value for automatic redirection. This response is cacheable unless indicated otherwise.

301 Moved Permanently

The requested resource has been assigned a new permanent URI and any future references to this resource SHOULD use one of the returned URIs. Clients with link editing capabilities ought to automatically re-link references to the Request-URI to one or more of the new references returned by the server, where possible. This response is cacheable unless indicated otherwise.

The new permanent URI SHOULD be given by the Location field in the response. Unless the request method was HEAD, the entity of the response SHOULD contain a short hypertext note with a hyperlink to the new URI(s).

If the 301 status code is received in response to a request other than GET or HEAD, the user agent MUST NOT automatically redirect the request unless it can be confirmed by the user, since this might change the conditions under which the request was issued.

302 Found

The requested resource resides temporarily under a different URI. Since the redirection might be altered on occasion, the client SHOULD continue to use the Request-URI for future requests. This response is only cacheable if indicated by a Cache-Control or Expires header field.

The temporary URI SHOULD be given by the Location field in the response. Unless the request method was HEAD, the entity of the response SHOULD contain a short hypertext note with a hyperlink to the new URI(s).

If the 302 status code is received in response to a request other than GET or HEAD, the user agent MUST NOT automatically redirect the request unless it can be confirmed by the user, since this might change the conditions under which the request was issued.

303 See Other

The response to the request can be found under a different URI and SHOULD be retrieved using a GET method on that resource. This method exists primarily to allow the output of a POST-activated script to redirect the user agent to a selected resource. The new URI is not a substitute reference for the originally requested resource. The 303 response MUST NOT be cached, but the response to the second (redirected) request might be cacheable.

The different URI SHOULD be given by the Location field in the response. Unless the request method was HEAD, the entity of the response SHOULD contain a short hypertext note with a hyperlink to the new URI(s).

304 Not Modified

If the client has performed a conditional GET request and access is allowed, but the document has not been modified, the server SHOULD respond with this status code. The 304 response MUST NOT contain a message-body, and thus is always terminated by the first empty line after the header fields.

If a clockless origin server obeys these rules, and proxies and clients add their own Date to any response received without one, caches will operate correctly.

If the conditional GET used a strong cache validator, the response SHOULD NOT include other entity-headers. Otherwise (i.e., the conditional GET used a weak validator), the response MUST NOT include other entity-headers; this prevents inconsistencies between cached entity-bodies and updated headers.

If a 304 response indicates an entity not currently cached, then the cache MUST disregard the response and repeat the request without the conditional.

If a cache uses a received 304 response to update a cache entry, the cache MUST update the entry to reflect any new field values given in the response.

305 Use Proxy

The requested resource MUST be accessed through the proxy given by the Location field. The Location field gives the URI of the proxy. The recipient is expected to repeat this single request via the proxy. 305 responses MUST only be generated by origin servers.

306 (Unused)

The 306 status code was used in a previous version of the specification, is no longer used, and the code is reserved.

307 Temporary Redirect

The requested resource resides temporarily under a different URI. Since the redirection MAY be altered on occasion, the client SHOULD continue to use the Request-URI for future requests. This response is only cacheable if indicated by a Cache-Control or Expires header field.

The temporary URI SHOULD be given by the Location field in the response. Unless the request method was HEAD, the entity of the response SHOULD contain a short hypertext note with a hyperlink to the new URI(s), since many pre-HTTP/1.1 user agents do not understand the 307 status. Therefore, the note SHOULD contain the information necessary for a user to repeat the original request on the new URI.

If the 307 status code is received in response to a request other than GET or HEAD, the user agent MUST NOT automatically redirect the request unless it can be confirmed by the user, since this might change the conditions under which the request was issued.

Client Error 4xx

The 4xx class of status code is intended for cases in which the client seems to have erred. Except when responding to a HEAD request, the server SHOULD include an entity containing an explanation of the error situation, and whether it is a temporary or permanent condition. These status codes are applicable to any request method. User agents SHOULD display any included entity to the user.

If the client is sending data, a server implementation using TCP SHOULD be careful to ensure that the client acknowledges receipt of the packet(s) containing the response, before the server closes the input connection. If the client continues sending data to the server after the close, the server's TCP stack will send a reset packet to the client, which may erase the client's unacknowledged input buffers before they can be read and interpreted by the HTTP application.

400 Bad Request

The request could not be understood by the server due to malformed syntax. The client SHOULD NOT repeat the request without modifications.

401 Unauthorized

The request requires user authentication. The response MUST include a WWW-Authenticate header field containing a challenge applicable to the requested resource. The client MAY repeat the request with a suitable Authorization header field. If the request already included Authorization credentials, then the 401 response indicates that authorization has been refused for those credentials. If the 401 response contains the same challenge as the prior response, and the user agent has already attempted authentication at least once, then the user SHOULD be presented the entity that was given in the response, since that entity might include relevant diagnostic information. HTTP access authentication is explained in "HTTP Authentication: Basic and Digest Access Authentication".

402 Payment Required

This code is reserved for future use.

403 Forbidden

The server understood the request, but is refusing to fulfill it. Authorization will not help and the request SHOULD NOT be repeated. If the request method was not HEAD and the server wishes to make public why the request has not been fulfilled, it SHOULD describe the reason for the refusal in the entity. If the server does not wish to make this information available to the client, the status code 404 (Not Found) can be used instead.

404 Not Found

The server has not found anything matching the Request-URI. No indication is given of whether the condition is temporary or permanent. The 410 (Gone) status code SHOULD be used if the server knows, through some internally configurable mechanism, that an old resource is permanently unavailable and has no forwarding address. This status code is commonly used when the server does not wish to reveal exactly why the request has been refused, or when no other response is applicable.

405 Method Not Allowed

The method specified in the Request-Line is not allowed for the resource identified by the Request-URI. The response MUST include an Allow header containing a list of valid methods for the requested resource.

406 Not Acceptable

The resource identified by the request is only capable of generating response entities which have content characteristics not acceptable according to the accept headers sent in the request.

Unless it was a HEAD request, the response SHOULD include an entity containing a list of available entity characteristics and location(s) from which the user or user agent can choose the one most appropriate. The entity format is specified by the media type given in the Content-Type header field. Depending upon the format and the capabilities of the user agent, selection of the most appropriate choice MAY be performed automatically. However, this specification does not define any standard for such automatic selection.

If the response could be unacceptable, a user agent SHOULD temporarily stop receipt of more data and query the user for a decision on further actions.

407 Proxy Authentication Required

This code is similar to 401 (Unauthorized), but indicates that the client must first authenticate itself with the proxy. The proxy MUST return a Proxy-Authenticate header field containing a challenge applicable to the proxy for the requested resource. The client MAY repeat the request with a suitable Proxy-Authorization header field. HTTP access authentication is explained in "HTTP Authentication: Basic and Digest Access Authentication".

408 Request Timeout

The client did not produce a request within the time that the server was prepared to wait. The client MAY repeat the request without modifications at any later time.

409 Conflict

The request could not be completed due to a conflict with the current state of the resource. This code is only allowed in situations where it is expected that the user might be able to resolve the conflict and resubmit the request. The response body SHOULD include enough information for the user to recognize the source of the conflict. Ideally, the response entity would include enough information for the user or user agent to fix the problem; however, that might not be possible and is not required.

Conflicts are most likely to occur in response to a PUT request. For example, if versioning were being used and the entity being PUT included changes to a resource which conflict with those made by an earlier (third-party) request, the server might use the 409 response to indicate that it can't complete the request. In this case, the response entity would likely contain a list of the differences between the two versions in a format defined by the response Content-Type.

410 Gone

The requested resource is no longer available at the server and no forwarding address is known. This condition is expected to be considered permanent. Clients with link editing capabilities SHOULD delete references to the Request-URI after user approval. If the server does not know, or has no facility to determine, whether or not the condition is permanent, the status code 404 (Not Found) SHOULD be used instead. This response is cacheable unless indicated otherwise.

The 410 response is primarily intended to assist the task of web maintenance by notifying the recipient that the resource is intentionally unavailable and that the server owners desire that remote links to that resource be removed. Such an event is common for limited-time, promotional services and for resources belonging to individuals no longer working at the server's site. It is not necessary to mark all permanently unavailable resources as "gone" or to keep the mark for any length of time—that is left to the discretion of the server owner.

411 Length Required

The server refuses to accept the request without a defined Content-Length. The client MAY repeat the request if it adds a valid Content-Length header field containing the length of the message-body in the request message.

412 Precondition Failed

The precondition given in one or more of the request-header fields evaluated to false when it was tested on the server. This response code allows the client to place preconditions on the current resource metainformation (header field data) and thus prevent the requested method from being applied to a resource other than the one intended.

413 Request Entity Too Large

The server is refusing to process a request because the request entity is larger than the server is willing or able to process. The server MAY close the connection to prevent the client from continuing the request.

If the condition is temporary, the server SHOULD include a Retry-After header field to indicate that it is temporary and after what time the client MAY try again.

414 Request-URI Too Long

The server is refusing to service the request because the Request-URI is longer than the server is willing to interpret. This rare condition is only likely to occur when a client has improperly converted a POST request to a GET request with long query information, when the client has descended into a URI "black hole" of redirection (e.g., a redirected URI prefix that points to a suffix of itself), or when the server is under attack by a client attempting to exploit security holes present in some servers using fixed-length buffers for reading or manipulating the Request-URI.

415 Unsupported Media Type

The server is refusing to service the request because the entity of the request is in a format not supported by the requested resource for the requested method.

416 Requested Range Not Satisfiable

A server SHOULD return a response with this status code if a request included a Range request-header field, and none of the range-specifier values in this field overlap the current extent of the selected resource, and the request did not include an If-Range request-header field. (For byte-ranges, this means that the first-byte-pos of all of the byte-range-spec values were greater than the current length of the selected resource.)

When this status code is returned for a byte-range request, the response SHOULD include a Content-Range entity-header field specifying the current length of the selected resource. This response MUST NOT use the multipart/byteranges content-type.

417 Expectation Failed

The expectation given in an Expect request-header field could not be met by this server, or, if the server is a proxy, the server has unambiguous evidence that the request could not be met by the next-hop server.

Server Error 5xx

Response status codes beginning with the digit "5" indicate cases in which the server is aware that it has erred or is incapable of performing the request. Except when responding to a HEAD request, the server SHOULD include an entity containing an explanation of the error situation, and whether it is a temporary or permanent condition. User agents SHOULD display any included entity to the user. These response codes are applicable to any request method.

500 Internal Server Error

The server encountered an unexpected condition which prevented it from fulfilling the request.

501 Not Implemented

The server does not support the functionality required to fulfill the request. This is the appropriate response when the server does not recognize the request method and is not capable of supporting it for any resource.

502 Bad Gateway

The server, while acting as a gateway or proxy, received an invalid response from the upstream server it accessed in attempting to fulfill the request.

503 Service Unavailable

The server is currently unable to handle the request due to a temporary overloading or maintenance of the server. The implication is that this is a temporary condition which will be alleviated after some delay. If known, the length of the delay MAY be indicated in a Retry-After header. If no Retry-After is given, the client SHOULD handle the response as it would for a 500 response.

504 Gateway Timeout

The server, while acting as a gateway or proxy, did not receive a timely response from the upstream server specified by the URI (e.g. HTTP, FTP, LDAP) or some other auxiliary server (e.g., DNS) it needed to access in attempting to complete the request.

505 HTTP Version Not Supported

The server does not support, or refuses to support, the HTTP protocol version that was used in the request message. The server is indicating that it is unable or unwilling to complete the request using the same major version as the client, other than with this error message. The response SHOULD contain an entity describing why that version is not supported and what other protocols are supported by that server.